A Student's Guide *to* Presentations

SAGE Essential Study Skills

Essential Study Skills is a series of books designed to help students and newly qualified professionals to develop their skills, capabilities, attitudes and qualities so that they can apply them intelligently and in ways which will benefit them on their courses and careers. The series includes accessible and user-friendly guides to improving a range of essential life-long skills and abilities in a variety of areas, including:

- writing essays and reports
- numeracy
- presenting information
- and communicating your ideas.

Essential Study Skills will be an invaluable aid to all students on a range of higher education courses and to professionals who need to make presentations, write effective reports or search for relevant information.

SAGE ESSENTIAL *Study Skills*

A Student's Guide *to* Presentations
Making your Presentation Count

Barbara Chivers and Michael Shoolbred

SAGE Publications
Los Angeles · London · New Delhi · Singapore

First published 2007

SAGE Publications Ltd
1 Oliver's Yard
55 City Road
London EC1Y 1SP

SAGE Publications Inc.
2455 Teller Road
Thousand Oaks, California 91320

SAGE Publications India Pvt Ltd
B I/I 1 Mohan Cooperative Industrial Area
Mathura Road
New Delhi 110 044

SAGE Publications Asia-Pacific Pte Ltd
33 Pekin Street #02-01
Far East Square
Singapore 048763

Library of Congress Control Number 2006940400

British Library Cataloguing in Publication data

A catalogue record for this book is available
from the British Library

ISBN 978-0-7619-4368-6
ISBN 978-0-7619-4369-3 (pbk)

Typeset by C&M Digitals (P) Ltd., Chennai, India
Printed in Great Britain by Athenaeum Press, Gateshead
Printed on paper from sustainable resources

Contents

List of Figures

List of Tables

Acknowledgements

Thank you to our persistent editors at Sage: Anna, Emily, Karen and Kate. Michael Shoolbred would like to thank the following who kindly allowed their material to be adapted for this book: Toni-Marie Daley, Malcolm Everett, Jayne Fellows, Clare Foster, Helen Hinks, Lisa Gregory, Vanessa Jones, Lyndsay Hope, Alison Parker, Andrew Shoolbred and Lizzie Shoolbred. Thanks to those others who commented on various chapters. Special thanks also to Rebecca Hartland-Fox.

Barbara Chivers would like to thank Mick for his continued support and Dan and Jake, who made her look at student presentations from a very different perspective.

We both appreciate the support and ideas given by: William Foster, Julie Pittaway, Ellen Thomson and Kate Williams.

We also wish to thank the many students involved in our research on interviews and presentation skills; without them this book would not have been possible.

We send our apologies to anyone left out!

Barbara Chivers and Michael Shoolbred
May 2007

Introduction

If you are a student in further or higher education and are sometimes asked to deliver presentations, you will find this book useful. Student presentations are used increasingly on educational courses to encourage students to be more active in their own learning. Many student presentations are used by tutors to assess student understanding, knowledge and progress in modules, and at important stages on academic and vocational courses. Presentations also help students to prepare for employment in organizations that place an increasing value on effective presentation skills. During the last few years we have noticed an increasing trend for presentations to be used by employers as part of their recruitment and selection procedures. This book aims to support you when you are preparing and delivering these presentations. We hope it will help you to cope with what is often a stressful part of your course.

How to use this book

We have tried to write this book in a style that is easy to read and understand. We realize that when you are busy preparing your presentations, most of your time will be used researching and reading about the topic, rather than on how to deliver good presentations. We also recognize that you will probably not be able to read the book in chapter order so each of the specialist chapters provides a concise guide to the theme and closes with a brief list of Key Principles for that theme. Frequent links are made between all chapters where they are relevant. We do suggest however, that you begin by reading Chapters 1 and 2 which provide a context for all of the other chapters.

Chapter summaries

- **Chapter 1 Why do a Presentation?** describes the many purposes, problems and benefits of student presentations. In the final part of this chapter, we outline six examples of student presentations. These are structured under several headings that will help you to identify parts of each example similar to your own experiences. You may be able to construct an example close to your own experience by using these different parts.
- **Chapter 2 What Makes an Effective Presentation?** outlines the characteristics of effective presentations and is intended to be used as an overview to encourage you to create a presentation that is effective, rather than just working to complete your presentation.

- **Chapter 3 Improving Individual Performance** suggests how to improve your own performance during presentations. This is a frequent cause of anxiety for students but this chapter will help you to become more confident.
- **Chapter 4 Presenting as Part of a Group** concentrates on how to work well in a group. Group presentations are used frequently on academic courses. This chapter explains the benefits and problems in group working and suggests techniques for working well together.
- **Chapter 5 Ten Steps for Preparing your Presentation** is a useful stand alone chapter on the tasks you need to work on to complete your presentation. It does however make useful links to all of the other chapters.
- **Chapter 6 Understanding your Audience** encourages you to think about who will be watching your presentation and why they are there. You may think this has little relevance to a student situation but we think you will find many useful points to consider in this chapter.
- **Chapter 7 Developing Content and Structure** advises you how to research and choose relevant content. It also discusses how to create a structure that helps the presentation to be understood by the audience.
- **Chapter 8 Creating Visual Aids and Handouts** discusses how you can use these items to improve your presentation.
- **Chapter 9 Using PowerPoint Effectively.** Many students overuse PowerPoint, resulting in tedious presentations. This chapter helps you to think about the best ways of using it to enhance rather than dominate your presentation.
- **Chapter 10 Learning from Presentations** explores how you can learn through delivering or watching presentations. Most presentations are used for some learning purpose and thinking about this will also help you to improve your communication and presentation skills.
- **Chapter 11 Delivering a Presentation as Part of an Interview** is the final chapter and has been included as a response to the increasing trend for including presentations as part of an interview for job recruitment. This chapter draws on student experiences to help you deliver effective presentations in an interview situation.
  We have included three Appendices.
- **Appendix 1 Presenting Numbers Effectively** provides a list of key points about how to use and present numeric data in your presentations.
- **Appendix 2 Copyright and Plagiarism** is a brief outline of the main points needed to comply with good academic practice.
- **Appendix 3 Presentation Skills Guidelines** is a useful checklist of key points from all of the chapters.

Finally, this book is a practical guide that is informed by our research and experience of working with students giving presentations for a variety of purposes. We hope the book helps you to enjoy giving presentations and to use them as opportunities for improving your knowledge and your communication and presentation skills. We welcome feedback on the contents with suggested improvements for future editions.

1 Why do a Presentation?

LEARNING OBJECTIVES

Reading this chapter will help you to:

- develop your understanding of the purposes of student presentations
- accept the benefits of delivering these presentations
- understand some of the reasons why presentations can be stressful
- recognize different examples of student presentations

This chapter provides a general overview of student presentations. Even though these presentations are very diverse, it is useful at this stage of the book to construct a general understanding of student presentations. We suggest that you read this chapter as an introduction to the book, before deciding which of the other chapters have relevance for your needs and situation.

Student presentations usually involve an individual or group of students presenting to academic staff, student peers or other invited audiences. Understanding the true purpose of your presentation can help you to prepare and deliver it more effectively.

Student presentations might include:

- Group and individual presentations for a given topic as part of a module assessment.
- Seminar presentations giving a paper to an academic or your peers for the purpose of teaching or showing evidence of your understanding of the topic.
- Providing an overview of some research carried out by you or your group.
- Demonstrating the use of a piece of equipment or software such as PowerPoint to show that you have developed the essential skills to use it appropriately.

- Dissertation-related presentations and Vivas to demonstrate your ability to manage a research project.
- A job interview where you have been asked to present for several minutes on a given topic.

We outline some examples of these later in the chapter. We hope you will find them useful for improving your understanding of the factors that need to be considered when developing your presentations. To help you achieve the learning objectives for this chapter we have divided it into four parts:

1   Purposes of student presentations.
2   Pressures and problems of giving presentations.
3   Benefits of student presentations.
4   Examples of student presentations.

1   Purposes of student presentations

There are many reasons why students are asked to give presentations and these will be influenced by your academic course and situational and organizational factors. The purpose and circumstances of your presentation will influence its style, content and structure. Most presentations will involve a combination of purposes but it may be helpful to think about the different features of each of these presentations.

Student presentations may be given for the purposes of:

- Advocacy/persuasion
- Training
- Teaching and learning
- Informing
- Assessment

By exploring these purposes, we can begin to understand the style that will need to be developed.

Advocacy/persuasion

This presentation usually involves persuading members of the audience to take some action or make a decision. Examples could include:

- support a cause
- join a student society

- vote for an individual to take up a role on a committee
- buy a product or service
- choose the best candidate for the job

This type of presentation will need a combination of relevant factual content delivered in a convincing and confident style. You will need to communicate clearly and succinctly. Some emotions such as enthusiasm or passion may be used in your delivery if you think this is appropriate, but you need to make sure that you do not embarrass yourself or the audience. You may also have to deal with some emotional reactions from the audience such as anger or ridicule. You will need to give a confident performance and deal effectively with their comments, manage the crowd and limit any negative reactions. As with all types of presentations it is crucial to keep control, especially when there are contributions and responses from the audience. We discuss this in more detail in Chapter 3. Example 6 at the end of this chapter involves some advocacy by persuading the recruitment panel that you are the best candidate for the job.

Training

This type of presentation includes examples where students may demonstrate their skills in the use of equipment and also their skills as a trainer or teacher. These types of presentations may be used to practise, demonstrate and eventually assess the level of these skills and techniques. Examples include:

- Demonstrating the use of a piece of equipment
- Demonstrating a medical procedure
- Training someone in the use of a software package
- Training a novice to use a piece of first aid equipment
- Demonstrating your communication skills as a trainer
- Demonstrating professional practice such as an interview technique, counselling skills or classroom management techniques.

In many vocational and professional courses, students have to learn the skills to use a range of equipment or demonstrate their communication skills. Presentations can also be used on these courses as opportunities for practice and rehearsal before the student is formally assessed and expected to perform in real life situations such as during their placements or probationary periods in employment.

Many first aid courses use this technique so that the participants can develop the key skills needed for proficiency. Health courses such as radiography are examples where the student will have to demonstrate the use of the equipment to a high level of proficiency before they work with patients.

Nurses and other health professionals need to learn the training techniques to communicate effectively on health promotion programmes. These techniques can be developed and practised in this type of presentation which can offer 'safe spaces' in which to develop these skills.

If you can think of presentations as opportunities for your own development, they may seem less daunting to you and indeed, this approach may help you to gain more benefit from preparing and delivering your presentations.

Immediate feedback can be an integral part of this type of presentation especially on the occasions when no formal assessment is given. The tutor may interrupt the session to ask for clarification or suggest an improvement that could be rehearsed several times until the student becomes more confident. Members of the audience may suggest ideas and changes for improvement. Role playing may be used so that students explore the skill or issue from a range of perspectives, then share ideas in a plenary session. Training presentations should result in learning for all the participants but we discuss this below. Examples 4 and 5, at the end of this chapter, are this type of presentation.

Teaching and learning

Almost all presentations should have some elements of teaching and learning as part of their purpose. However for the purposes of this book it is useful to explore this as a specific purpose and to do this we have chosen a few examples where presentations are used for:

- Developing a deeper understanding of a topic or text
- Covering specific areas of the curriculum in more detail
- Explaining an experiment or cooking process
- Inviting a visiting expert to speak on a given topic

The content of this presentation is usually focused on a topic area relevant to a course or module being studied. This may involve new research and knowledge that extends how the topic has previously been taught by the tutors. It may also involve 'repackaging' knowledge already covered or further exploration of the topic by looking at different perspectives. An example of this could be where a group of students are asked to present on the topic 'Globalization' from the different perspectives of a farmer in a developing country, a small manufacturing organization in England and a multinational organization that has offices on four continents. Sometimes, these types of student presentations are used to explore areas of a curriculum in greater detail than has been covered in lectures. This helps the presenters to develop deeper knowledge and the audience to broaden their understanding of the topic and may be the reason why the academic has included presentations in the module. All of the examples at the end of this chapter incorporate some teaching and learning but Examples 2, 3 and 4 have a strong teaching and learning purpose.

Informing

In some circumstances this could be seen as similar to teaching but the aim of this type of presentation could be to communicate as much information as possible in the time available. The purpose of the presentation may be to:

* Describe a new policy
* Outline a set of instructions
* Give a progress report on some research or development

This type of presentation is used in many organizations where students or employees are expected to report progress at key stages of a project. It provides evidence of ongoing work and can be used as a subtle measure of control where individuals work to meet deadlines set for the submission dates for these progress reports. Many employers expect academic courses to have provided opportunities for students to develop their presentation skills so that they could communicate effectively in the organizational environment.

For a student situation, a Viva could have this purpose where the function is to present your research aims and results then answer questions from the audience. Examples 1 and 5 in this chapter describe this type of presentation.

Assessment

Student presentations are frequently assessed and may be awarded a percentage of the marks that contribute to the overall module mark and credits. However, some presentations may not be assessed but used as an opportunity for students to practise and further develop their presentation skills, without the anxiety of earning marks for the quality of their performance. There is a tension here for students, as most presentations need quite a lot of preparation time. This time may only be seen as worthwhile if it earns marks towards the completion of a unit or module of study. Equally, it can influence students to withdraw from non-assessed presentations or use a minimum of effort for such events, seeing them as less important for their learning and achievement. This focus on marks earned, rather than expe-rience gained, may influence some tutors to only use assessed presentations.

Use of assessment can have a positive advantage. For some students, presentations offer opportunities to earn a higher proportion of marks than they might achieve for the written part of their assessment. They may be better communicators and presenters in their use of speech, visuals or technology than in a written mode. These students may feel they need this book less for the general ideas about presentation skills but can use it more for the suggestions about content development. We cover assessment in all the examples at the end of this chapter but discuss assessment in more detail in Chapter 9.

2   Pressures and problems of giving presentations

We intend this book to provide you with positive advice and encouragement but we do recognize that presentations are not always popular with students. We think it will be useful to outline some of the problems to reduce or even remove your fears.

- **I would prefer to write an essay rather than deliver a presentation!**
  You may think presentations are more difficult to deliver than having to complete an essay or report for an assignment. They can certainly increase your anxiety levels and you may think that you actually have to work harder for a presentation than for an assignment. Whilst this may not be true, your higher anxiety levels may cause you to believe this and you may not use your time as effectively in the preparation, because of this anxiety.

  You may feel more nervous about reading your work aloud in a presentation than the more private situation where an academic reads your written work alone and no-one from your peer group sees the quality of your work.

  We discuss how to deal with this in Chapters 3 and 5. You might also find some useful advice in Chapter 6.

- **I only seem to learn from the content of my own presentations but not when I have to listen to other students. There is no point attending the other presentations!**
  This is a frequent complaint from students and a real challenge to academics for how to use presentations as a good learning experience for everyone involved. We hope that using this book will help to eliminate this attitude but it is useful to remember that if you feel like this, so will your audience, therefore, think about what you can do to make sure that they learn something from your presentation and find it interesting! Chapter 10 will be useful to help with this problem. Chapter 6 provides some useful tips for keeping the audience involved and Chapter 7 will encourage you to think about developing content that is interesting and relevant to modules being studied.

- **I do not know enough about the topic to give a presentation!**
  Presentations can also be stressful if you are asked to present on a topic about which you have only a limited knowledge. In these situations you may need to use a large amount of preparation time to develop new knowledge before you feel confident enough to prepare and plan the presentation. Whilst you may see this as stressful and

a disadvantage of presentations, in some circumstances, this is exactly why they are chosen as a method of assessment. They force you to develop new knowledge and to prepare well for the event. Use Chapter 5 to help you with this.

- **There is so much information on the topic I cannot decide what to include and what to leave out!**
  In this situation, you may feel overwhelmed by the size of the topic and experience feelings of panic when you have to make decisions about the content. There will probably be some guidance and advice in tutorials to help you decide what to include and what to leave out. Chapter 7 will also help you to cope with this situation.

- **I am nervous of using technology in public**
  To some extent, this is less of a problem for the younger students who will probably have developed higher levels of ICT skills at school, compared with mature students who may be less experienced. Using technology may be a real problem for mature students. Some presentations are designed to provide opportunities for practice. We outline an example of this within the purposes section on Training, earlier in this chapter. Chapters 8 and 9 will also be useful to help you deal with this problem and will help you to use technology to improve the presentation.

- **I am always nervous about speaking in a public situation**
  Most people feel nervous about the public performance required for a presentation, even if the audience is only one or two people instead of a larger group. Whilst good preparation and rehearsal will help to reduce some of the nerves, it is only through practice that you will learn to use your nervousness in a positive way that helps your performance. Chapter 3 gives some useful tips. Some students say they feel more nervous when presenting to other students on their courses than when presenting to people who they do not know such as for a job interview. You may find it useful to think about whether judgment by your peers may seem more daunting than by strangers. Whichever preference you have, we discuss how to deal with an audience in Chapter 6.

- **Group presentations are usually a problem. I feel that I do more of the work than other group members!**
  You may experience higher anxiety levels preparing for and delivering a group presentation than for an individual presentation. Problems with group behaviour may divert attention away from the real preparation tasks and more time can be spent arguing or discussing what needs to be done instead of actually doing the work needed to complete the preparation. These are discussed in Chapter 4 which offers suggestions for how to work well together.

- **I think I could earn higher marks for an individual presentation than for a group presentation!**
  Sometimes this is experienced by students who have previously had problems working for a group presentation. You may believe that you could earn higher marks because you are more capable than other group members, or that the group pressures divert energy away from good content development. Whilst this may be true in some

situations, many tutors use group presentations as opportunities to develop the team working and project management skills that many employers say are essential in the workplace. On many academic courses the assessment procedures are monitored and adjusted to make sure that final marks reflect the true ability of the individual student rather than the group members, so a group mark may only be a small proportion of the total marks for the module.

In spite of these concerns, presentations are a frequent experience in education and you will probably have to deliver several on your courses, so it is useful to recognize the benefits as well as the problems. When presentations have been completed, students frequently claim to have enjoyed the experience and report feelings of exhilaration and a sense of achievement. We discuss these benefits briefly below.

3   Benefits of student presentations

As with the variety of purposes, the benefits of student presentations will be influenced by the situation but they can be summarized as providing opportunities for:

- Student-centred participation in their learning
- Developing new knowledge and different perspectives on a topic
- Practice in a known environment/situation
- Increasing confidence to speak and present in front of an audience
- Improving marks earned for a module assessment
- Developing a wide range of communication and presentation skills
- Preparation for skills needed in the workplace
- An exchange of roles and perspectives from audience to presenter

Student-centred participation in their learning

Presentations offer variety and challenges that contrast with regular delivery by an academic lecturer. Students can sometimes be more willing to learn from the poor and good performances of their peers than from their tutors. Presentations can also be used as an effective form of peer learning. By taking responsibility for preparing and delivering a presentation, you take an active role in the process of your learning.

Develop new knowledge and perspectives on a topic

Presentations offer opportunities for developing skills and knowledge together. This process can strengthen learning and enthusiasm for further knowledge. If the presentation is effective, the audience should have learned something new and increased their interest about the topic. We sometimes remember information when we have heard it from an unusual source or one that is different. Tutors can learn new ideas from student perspectives which can influence their teaching and delivery.

Practise in a known environment/situation

Presentations offer opportunities for students to practise performing in a fairly safe environment. When you have to prepare several presentations on a course, you will begin to develop the essential skills and transfer these from presentation to presentation. The academic environment will probably be familiar to you. You might present in rooms where you attend lectures and other events and this can help to reduce some of your anxiety. If the audience is made up of other members of your cohort, they may be supportive because they can empathize with your feelings.

Increasing confidence to speak and present in front of an audience

Well-managed presentations, as part of academic courses, can be used developmentally to improve both skills and confidence levels. You may be able to demonstrate your personality in a way that is not possible as a passive listener in a lecture. Presentations can help you to be noticed and stand out from the rest of the group. They enable you to show your individuality. You can learn to deal with nervousness in a positive way that can help to reduce your fears and anxieties. With regular practice, you will improve your confidence and enter employment with some of the interpersonal and communication skills that employers value.

Improving marks earned for a module assessment

Sometimes, presentations give you opportunities for earning a higher percentage of marks than for written work alone. Students who prefer to speak rather than write, may be better communicators and presenters in their use of speech or visuals than in a written mode. This is because presentations use different intelligences in addition to the linguistic intelligence needed for essays and reports. In our experience some students are quite confident for their presentations and work better in group situations than on their own. These students may earn a higher total mark for the module where there is a combined assessment of presentation and written report, especially when the presentation earns up to 40 per cent of the module mark.

Developing a wide range of communication and presentation skills

You may need to think about your own skills and preferences for how you communicate. Do you prefer charts and graphs, diagrams or text, mind maps or lists? Presentations can help you to communicate using different media formats. They also give you opportunities to practise performing in public and develop your speech, use of hands and breathing, all of which we discuss in Chapter 3. Students in the audience will also watch and learn from the presenters' skills, especially if an opportunity is provided to comment on the presentation. Indeed, students are often highly critical of their own performance and that of their peers. These observations and criticisms can provide useful reflection and recognition of what makes presentations an effective learning situation for them. This reflection can improve future performances and be used in the wider application of job interviews and appraisals.

Preparation for skills needed in the workplace

Many employers seek confident candidates and use presentations as a part of their selection procedures. Some organizations use staff presentations frequently for progress reports, staff appraisal and development. Preparing and delivering presentations as a student can help you to be a more competent and confident candidate for interviews. They offer opportunities to develop your team working and project management skills. You will have to work to deadlines and take responsibility for delivering an outcome of your work. You will improve your research, design and communication skills as well as your general presentation skills. We encourage you to see student presentations as positive experiences that help to prepare you for future employment.

4   Examples of student presentations

You may find it useful to read through the examples provided below. These examples are used in later chapters where we discuss some of their features in more detail and provide some useful tips for delivering effective presentations. These examples are:

1   A Viva to present an overview of your research
2   A seminar presentation
3   A group presentation on a topic allocated to the group
4   A demonstration of your skills in using equipment
5   Non-assessed presentations to report research progress or demonstrate your product
6   An individual presentation for a job interview

Even if your presentation situation does not match these examples exactly, you will be able to see some features that are similar to your own experience. To help you identify their relevance, we have structured each example under the same headings for easy comparison. You could use these headings as a template to think about the different features of your own presentations. These headings form a useful acronym PACTHATC:

- Purpose
- Assessment
- Content
- Timing
- Handouts
- Audience
- Technology
- Comment

Example 1: a Viva to present an overview of your research

Purpose   All students are final year undergraduates presenting the research they have carried out for their dissertation.

Assessment   This Viva will be assessed to earn a percentage of marks that contribute towards your degree classification. The percentage varies across courses and could range from 10–40 per cent. A small proportion will be for your presentation skills but the majority of the marks will be given for the quality of research and your understanding of the subject area.

Content   This should consist of a brief outline of the research aims and objectives and the methods used. However, the main part of the presentation should concentrate on the results, conclusions and recommendations for future research. At the end you will be asked questions about different aspects of your research to test your knowledge and understanding of what has been achieved.

Timing   One hour has been allocated for each student presentation. Within this time, you will need to enter the room, load any PowerPoint presentation, present the content for about 20 minutes, answer questions for up to 30 minutes, pack up and leave the room. If time runs out you will lose marks for poor structure and time management.

Handouts   These must be provided for panel members and will probably consist of a copy of the slides used plus additional notes that you think are important. These need to be of a high standard as they could be used in the panel discussion after you have left the room and may have a small influence on the final mark.

Audience   This is a panel of three people, two will be academics. One is your Dissertation Tutor. You may have been taught by the other academic who is in the same teaching department as your tutor. The third person is an external visitor who could be either an academic from another organization or a professional practitioner. The panel will probably have agreed their questions before the start of the Viva but there will be freedom and flexibility for them to explore the themes that emerge during your presentation. This means that the direction of the questions can be uncertain and you will need to be knowledgeable and confident enough to guide their questions to areas that you consider to be most useful or beneficial to your performance.

Technology   You will be expected to use the most appropriate technology such as PowerPoint, audio, video or any kit that needs to be demonstrated.

Comment   This Viva will be an important event in your course. You will have worked hard on your research and this is your opportunity to demonstrate the quality of your research and your understanding and enthusiasm for the topic area. You will have only a short amount of time to get your message across to the audience. At this final stage of the course you will have deeper knowledge and be very 'close' to the research so that preparing the presentation might be difficult. You will need to step back and be objective about what is the most useful content that conveys the level of work in such a short amount of time. However, this could be an opportunity to explain and justify what was not articulated in the dissertation. It might be possible to find out who the panel members are beforehand and this could help you to focus the content on specific themes, especially if they are experts in the topic area of the presentation.

Example 2: A seminar presentation

Purpose   You are asked to give a paper to your tutor and your student cohort. The purpose of the seminar is for you to provide evidence of your research for and understanding of the topic or the text. Also, in this situation, you take some responsibility for teaching the other students who attend the seminar. They are expected to understand the content and use it elsewhere in the module when it is relevant.

Assessment   For this presentation you earn a fixed amount of marks that are 15 per cent of the module total but completing the seminar to a 'reasonable standard' earns the marks rather than marks being awarded for content and performance. However, if the tutor judges it to be of a low standard and of limited value, you will be asked to deliver it again on another occasion. This is to ensure that students work towards an acceptable standard of preparation and delivery. However, a similar example could be developed where you earn an individual mark within the 15 per cent that reflects your skills and performance in the seminar.

Content   You have been briefed about the text or the topic areas to be covered by the academic tutor. You have to provide an overview of the text or topic then explore key themes in more detail. The tutor has been available to offer guidance and you have reported your progress and asked any questions through e-mails.

Timing   The seminar will last for one hour. This will consist of approximately 40 minutes for your presentation and the remaining 20 minutes for questions and discussion. You are free to decide how and when you allow the questions to be asked. The tutor may interrupt during the seminar to ask you for further explanation and may direct the questions to ensure that relevant themes and issues have been covered.

Handouts   You are expected to provide some handouts that explain the topic as it will not be covered in detail in any other seminars or lectures on the module. These could be a copy of your script for the seminar. Alternatively, they could be a list of the main themes in your content, with brief descriptions, examples, facts and key issues relating to the topic. Both types of handouts should include references to useful resources that can be followed up at a later date.

Audience   This will be the module tutor and student members of the cohort so it could range between four and 20+ people.

Technology   Use of technology will vary between giving a handout that is used to direct the structure of the seminar to use of PowerPoint to cover the content.

Comment   In this example, your presentation skills are not directly assessed but you will be expected to deliver the content in a clear style that generates interest in the topic. Probably much of the preparation time will have been spent reading so that you understand the topic or text well enough to present a seminar from which the other students can learn. You will need to develop a logical structure that explores key themes and draws some conclusions. The quality of your performance in this seminar will develop your reputation for delivering good or poor quality seminars. The audience will feel more positive towards you if they leave with some useful notes and a deeper understanding of the topic and consider their time to have been well spent!

Example 3: Group presentation on a topic allocated to the group

Purpose   This presentation provides an opportunity to research and provide a more detailed review of an area of the curriculum covered in the general lectures. You are expected to draw on themes covered throughout the module to demonstrate how well you understand the topic. The audience will be expected to learn more about the topic by listening to the presentation. Thus it combines several purposes of teaching, learning and assessment.

Assessment   This presentation earns a percentage of marks that contribute towards the overall module mark. The percentage varies across courses and could range from 10–50 per cent. How these marks are given will vary with the situation but they could be given for your presentation skills, the quality of your research, your understanding of the subject area and perhaps the supporting handouts. In some presentations, marks may also be given for how well you work as a group. All members of the group will be given the same mark so you might be concerned that you will be limited by the weaker members of the group. There will however, be an opportunity to earn the remaining percentage through your individual piece of work.

Content   The topic areas to be covered have been allocated by the tutor. You have to provide an overview of the topic then explore key themes in more detail. The tutor has been available to offer guidance and you have reported your progress and asked any questions through e-mails.

Timing   A fixed amount of time will have been allocated for this presentation. The time could be between 20 and 60 minutes. A small proportion of this time will be devoted to questions from the audience.

Handouts   You are expected to provide some handouts that explain the topic as it will not be covered in detail in any other seminars or lectures on the module. These should be more than just copies of any slides used and could be notes from part of the script for the presentation or summaries of key themes with references to useful resources that can be followed up at a later date.

Audience   This will be the module tutor and student members of your cohort so it could perhaps be up to 40 people. They will probably have a general understanding of the topic but apart from the tutor, they will not be experts.

Technology   You will be expected to use the most appropriate technology such as PowerPoint, audio or video.

Comment   In this example, you will be expected to work well as a group. Your presentation skills will be assessed and you will be expected to deliver the content in a clear style that generates interest in the topic. Probably much of the preparation time will have been spent researching and reading so that you understand the topic well enough to deliver a presentation from which the other students can learn. Time will also be needed to allocate tasks between the group members and share the responsibility for preparing the content, designing the handouts and practising the content. You will need to develop a presentation that has a logical structure and interesting content that explore key themes and draw some conclusions.

Example 4: A demonstration of your skills in using equipment

Purpose   This type of presentation is an opportunity to demonstrate your current level of skill in using some equipment so that the tutor can give advice on how to improve these skills. This equipment will be something that you will be expected to use competently in your future employment. This could be in a medical context or craft design or technology courses. First aid training could be another example where dummies are substituted for people. Other examples could include: hairdressing, cookery, car maintenance, laboratory work. The purpose is to show the tutor your skills, plus you will have the opportunity for further learning and improvement of these skills.

Assessment   This is not assessed as a presentation. You will have some formal assessment in the future before you become a practitioner so this presentation will be useful as a form of rehearsal and training before the final assessed presentation.

Content   You will need to explain the context for the use of the equipment and demonstrate the correct use. You may also need to outline some examples of variations of its use such as for different patients or different medical conditions. If it is a laboratory situation, you may also need to explain safety precautions or how problems and mistakes can be rectified.

Timing   The time may vary between 10 and 60 minutes depending on the type of demonstration. Some time for feedback will be included so that areas for further practice can be discussed and agreed.

Handouts   These may not be needed for this type of presentation. However, you may be asked to provide a set of instructions for demonstrating the equipment as the process of creating these instructions will improve your understanding of the techniques needed.

Audience   The tutor will be present but there may also be other members of your cohort as this can be a useful learning event through the chance to observe the procedure and discuss aspects that arise from the demonstration.

Technology   The technology will be central to the purpose of this type of presentation rather than a communication tool or enhancement. This will vary depending on any of the examples given above such as the use of a dummy for a first aid course, engineering equipment or a sewing machine on a craft course.

Comment   Do not think that because there is no formal assessment, you do not need to prepare for this type of presentation. You will need to work and rehearse as for any others. This presentation offers an opportunity for some coaching and learning. It is really useful to demonstrate your level of skill and where you are having any problems with the technology. The tutor will advise you on how to improve and may give tips to solve any problems.

Example 5: non-assessed presentations to report progress or demonstrate a product

Purpose   There are two presentations in this example. You are a member of a group that has to design a website for the final assessment of a module. (On some courses this could be a garment, prototype, recipe or other relevant product.) You also have to write an individual report about the development of the site and discuss the reasons for choice of features and content. Halfway through the assignment, everyone in the group has to meet the tutor for an informal presentation on the progress of your work. The idea is that the presentation will inform the tutor of the progress you have made, so that she can advise you on any problems. This is similar to the previous example where the tutor will advise and encourage the students to improve their product for the final assessment. At the end of the module the completed website (product) will be demonstrated by the group.

Assessment   Neither of these presentations will be formally assessed. You will be given an individual mark for your own final report and a separate mark for the website that you develop as a group. It is therefore in your interest to create a good product with the group but also produce a high quality individual report so that you earn a good combined mark for the assignment. Whilst this presentation will not earn a mark it should contribute to your final mark if you use it wisely. Having a date for the presentation can help group members to focus on tasks that need to be developed. You will also be able to explain any problems that have arisen and seek some advice and suggestions from the tutor. The final presentation can be used to 'sell' the product and convince the tutor of the quality of the website or product. This will be important if it could influence the final mark given to the product.

Content   For the first presentation, you only have a few minutes to explain your ideas clearly. You will explain your progress so far, any problems you are having and how you see the product developing. This will be interactive as your group and the tutor will be able to ask questions about the product. The second presentation will be more formal as you will explain and demonstrate the completed site. The tutor will ask questions at the end of the presentation and make notes that will help later when she marks the site and the individual reports.

Timing   You are going to be allowed about 10 minutes for the first presentation and 45 minutes for the second one.

Handouts   For the first presentation you will probably only need notes of the work in progress that show tasks and proposed time scales that can be reviewed by the academic. However, clear detailed notes that perhaps include diagrams will help to keep you working well towards the goal. For the second presentation you are asked to demonstrate the product and give a brief outline report of the key features of the product and anticipated users. This report will be included as part of each of the group members' final individual reports that will also include critical analysis and reflections on the processes used and features of the product that could be improved further.

Audience   The presentation is to the tutor but other members of the cohort are supposed to be present, so that they see the products created by other students, and learn by observing their peers' performance.

Technology   This will be the software package used to develop the website.

Comment   In this example, you need good presentation and communication skills but they are not directly assessed. You may not feel very motivated because you know that you will not get a specific mark for the presentation. It is important to see this as an opportunity to practise in a non-threatening context, then to convince the tutor of the merits of your product.

Example 6: an individual presentation for a job interview

Purpose   You are one of six candidates in the final selection group for a job. You are asked to attend a final interview where you will meet the recruitment panel to answer questions about the skills that you can bring to the job. You have also been asked to prepare a 10 minute presentation on a given topic using PowerPoint. This presentation is one of several methods used to select the most suitable candidate but it is your opportunity to demonstrate your presentation skills, levels of confidence, personality and interpersonal skills.

Assessment   The panel will use a scoring system for the presentation of each candidate, but you will not be given this score. They understand that you will be nervous but will award marks for: keeping within the brief given; selection of relevant content; clarity of communication skills; appropriate use of PowerPoint. The quality of the presentation will contribute towards a final score of marks earned for group exercises and psychometric tests which will also be used in the selection process. However, where these scores are similar between candidates, the presentation will probably influence the final choice. It is therefore an important method within this range of selection methods.

Content   You have been given a topic or statement relevant to the type of job you have applied for. In a short presentation it is essential to be very succinct. However it can still be useful to provide a brief introduction to the content, structure the main part into three broad themes and then close the presentation.

Timing   A fixed amount of time has been allocated for each candidate and the 10 minute presentation is part of this. The panel members will be able to question you after the presentation and this could take up to 20 minutes. After you leave the room, they will discuss your performance and agree the final mark.

Handouts   You have been asked to provide a handout of the set of slides used with space for notes at the side. Panel members will use these to make the notes needed to remind them of your performance when they are comparing you with the other candidates.

Audience   This will be members of the recruitment panel and there may also be several of the team of people who the successful candidate will be working with. You will not have met any of these people before the interview; neither will you be able to visit the place of the presentation before the event. The panel make the decision for offering you the job or rejecting you as unsuitable for the post.

Technology   You have been informed about the levels and type of technology available. You have been asked to e-mail the file to a specific address the day before the interview but will have also been advised to bring a copy on disc in case of unforeseen problems with the organization's intranet.

Comment   In this example you need to make an impact and get your message across in a short amount of time. You will be expected to 'sell' yourself by using good presentation skills to show your potential as a strong candidate for the job. Somehow, you need to be better than the other candidates. Inevitably you will also be judged on your appearance and how they see you as capable of representing their organization in a positive way. Read Chapter 11 for more about this type of presentation.

Conclusion

Having read this chapter, you will now be aware of a range of examples of student presentations, why they are used, and the problems and benefits you can experience from delivering presentations. We hope you find the rest of this book helpful for preparing and delivering all of your presentations.

2 What Makes an Effective Presentation?

LEARNING OBJECTIVES

Reading this chapter will help you to:

- understand the concept of effective presentations
- list the characteristics that contribute to effective presentations
- recognize how each characteristic contributes to the overall effectiveness of your presentation

What are effective presentations?

Effective presentations achieve their objectives and usually bring some benefit and learning to all the people involved in them, whether presenters, audience or tutors. They will also earn good marks if they are assessed. Presentations need to be interesting and useful to the learning situation but they can also be enjoyable, even memorable. You may remember more of the content of your peers' presentations than the content delivered by the lecturers. You may also remember the content of your own presentations more than the content of lectures you have attended. This may be because of the anxiety levels associated with presentations and the amount of preparation and rehearsal time needed for the content to be developed.

We have chosen the following characteristics of effective presentations. These have been identified through research with several cohorts of our students and through our own experience of developing and assessing student presentations as assignments on their academic courses. These characteristics are given in the order of preparing and delivering the presentation rather than in any order of importance.

- Careful planning and preparation
- Good time management

- Relevant and interesting content
- Clear structure
- Good communication skills
- Appropriate use of technologies
- Clear supporting documentation
- Suitable audience participation

All of these will apply to a greater or lesser extent depending on your situation and the purpose of your presentation. We suggest that you read and review the detail of each characteristic noting the points you think are most relevant for you. Cross-references are provided to the chapters that provide further detail and advice.

Careful planning and preparation

Planning and preparation usually involve some research and choosing or rejecting suitable content. These are important tasks which will probably take much longer than you first thought. It is outside the scope of this book to discuss research techniques in any depth but it is useful to recognize here that research does take time and may involve some of the following activities before content can be chosen, created and presented:

- searching databases and on-line resources for articles
- use of libraries for reviewing relevant resources
- tutorials with academic staff to develop new knowledge
- contact with and visits to organizations
- interviews with experts
- construction and testing of models
- developing experiments and analysing results

This all sounds daunting but we list these to encourage you to see the presentation as the end-product of a range of tasks carried out, rather than as a single event. The type and level of your course of study will almost certainly influence the type of preparation needed as will the amount of marks to be earned and credits that can be achieved. Chapter 5 outlines 10 steps for the planning and preparation stage.

Good time management

Time management is important for preparing and delivering good presentations yet it is often a source of stress for students. For your presentation, good time management is important in two quite different ways: in the planning and preparation stages; and time allocated for delivering the presentation.

1   Planning and preparation stages   In some situations you may have just a few days to prepare for the presentation, for others you may be given several weeks. Each brings benefits and problems. A short amount of time creates pressures on what you can achieve and may limit the quality of the final presentation. A longer amount of time can result in a lack of focus with tasks being left until closer to the delivery date, then a period of frenzied activity leading up to the event. However much time you are given to prepare, you may find it useful to create a time plan or a chart of your intended progress. This could involve:

- listing all of the tasks that need to be completed before the date of the presentation
- placing these tasks in an order of priority
- allocating the time needed to complete each of these tasks
- checking your progress regularly
- reallocating the remaining time to make sure that you complete all of the tasks

Time will probably be needed for reading to increase your understanding of the topic. However, to be able to present, explain or teach that content to someone else in the audience needs even deeper levels of understanding and this will probably use quite a large amount of your preparation time.

If you are part of a group, some planning meetings will need to be arranged and communication through e-mails set up. Time will also be needed for preparing and testing visuals, models or demonstration materials and for rehearsing the use of technologies. Handouts and other supporting documents may need to be compiled, edited and copies made. See Chapters 7, 8 and 9 for more detailed discussion on these tasks.

It is also important to allow for some rehearsal time to ensure a more polished performance and greater confidence. This is especially important for a group presentation where timing will be important. We discuss this briefly below, and in more detail in Chapters 3 and 4.

2   Time allocated for delivering the presentation   In most presentations, it is usually better to deliver less content at a reasonable pace, than too much content at a faster pace that may leave the audience feeling overwhelmed and confused. How you use the time during the presentation will be influenced by how much content you intend to cover, the structure of this content and the amount of audience participation expected. Also, how you create and use the supporting documentation will influence how you make use of the time during your presentation. If time is short, you could cover a few important points at a general level during the presentation then suggest that the audience read the more detailed handouts in their own time.

Allocating and managing the performance time can be even more of a problem for a group presentation. In some situations where several group presentations will be given in a fixed amount of time, the tutor may stop the presentation when the allotted time has been used, regardless of how much of the presentation has been delivered. If this happens, you will almost certainly lose marks or be penalized in some way.

This emphasizes the importance of rehearsing and editing. During rehearsal, each person will need to be timed so that time for one part of the presentation is not somehow used by one of the other presenters. If each presenter is allocated five minutes for their part, they should be timed during the rehearsals so that some changes can be made if they overrun. We discuss group work in more detail in Chapter 4.

If you are delivering the presentation alone, you will probably be judged on how the time has been used. Has there been enough time for the difficult content or was so much time used at the start on the preliminary information and the most important content appears rushed and too brief? As you develop the content you will probably become more certain about the best use of the time and the tutor may give you some guidance on this in a tutorial.

Remember that if you are one of several presentations at a conference or with other members of your cohort, you will not be popular for overrunning on your time slot. The time will need to be recovered probably from another presentation or from social time such as refreshment or activity breaks. In an interview situation, how close you keep to the time allocated to each candidate may earn you marks. Overrunning may cause you to lose a few marks!

Relevant and interesting content

You may find it useful to create the content in the following ways:

- decide what to include and what to leave out
- choose examples to provide interest and improve understanding
- provide links to further sources of information

Decide what to include and what to leave out　For many subject areas there is usually much more content than can be delivered within the time allocated for the presentation. You will need to set your chosen content within the context of the module studied and make sure that it is relevant, accurate and interesting to the audience. It might be useful in your introduction to outline the reasons for your choice of content and the emphasis of the presentation. If you have enough time, it could also be useful to explain very briefly how other content was considered and why it was rejected.

Choose examples to provide interest and improve understanding   There is a lot of research evidence that shows how using examples improves our understanding and learning. You will need to think about how to use examples in the presentation and where to place them in the structure of the content.

You can use examples to explain how they improved your own understanding of the topic. Remember, if you found examples helped your own understanding, this will probably be the same for your audience. How you use the examples is usually very important when the presentation is assessed and a portion of the marks may be given for how examples are used. Think about using them in a critical and analytical way, instead of just describing them. Just listing or describing some examples can become tedious for the audience.

It can be helpful at the start of a presentation to use examples that the audience will already understand. This helps them to review their existing knowledge. You can then move on to use new and perhaps more complex examples to extend their thinking. Also, think about how you can use some topical examples to keep their interest and attention. Remember, however relevant or important the content is to the purpose of the presentation, it could still be incredibly boring for the audience to listen to.

Provide links to further sources of information   It is usually helpful to provide links to useful sources of information that audience members can follow up in their own time. These sources could relate to content that you have not been able to include but can be used for further reading and knowledge development.

You may also give links to useful websites and perhaps give some brief evaluation for why a source is especially useful. Use this approach to save their time yet indicate the volume and type of information that is available. Even if you only provide this type of information in the handouts, it shows evidence of your own research and may be useful to some members of the audience in the future. See Chapters 7 and 8 for more discussion on these suggestions.

Clear structure

A clear structure usually helps the audience to gain a quick understanding of the content of the presentation. Provide a clear outline or overview of the presentation so that they understand the progression of the topic and how it relates to a wider picture. Links can be made to what the audience already know and understand. It may also be helpful to tell them what you expect them to understand by the end of the presentation by stating your aims and objectives at the start. This is especially important in academic presentations where learning outcomes may also need to be identified.

Provide a brief but clear introduction to the topic. Divide the content to be covered into sections that are relevant to the knowledge but that also enable pauses for reflection and opportunities for reviewing key issues. Provide links between the different sections then draw the presentation to a conclusion, perhaps by reviewing the themes covered, summarizing results or emphasizing the most important points or future issues and concerns.

There is much research evidence to show that we recall and remember more detail from the beginning and ending of presentations and lectures than in the middle. This can be problematic as the deep content may be placed in this middle part. There are techniques that can help you with this and we discuss them in more detail in Chapter 7. However, the general advice is to use several beginnings and endings throughout the presentation by structuring the content well and changing the approach or activity periodically to keep the attention of the audience. Opportunities for this approach will be limited in a short presentation but the principles still apply and being aware of these techniques emphasizes the importance of having a clear structure.

Good communication skills

For communication to be effective, the content needs to be clearly understood, meaningful and interesting to the audience. Effective communication in presentations needs a combination of content that fits the purpose, and good presentation and communication skills. To achieve this, you will need to consider several questions:

- What is the purpose of the presentation and what is it that you need to communicate in the allotted time?
- What is the current knowledge level of the audience and what new knowledge or awareness do you want the audience to have gained from listening to or seeing your presentation?
- What is the most effective way to communicate this knowledge? For example, is it more useful to show pictures, use models, sound, speech or text?

There are many influences on how well we communicate and on how well we are understood by our audience. It is useful to consider these influences under three broad areas:

1 Verbal communications.
2 Visual communications.
3 Non-verbal communications.

*1   **Verbal communications***   We suggest five principles here:

- ***Limit your use of jargon.*** Generally speaking, to be understood, the presenter needs to use vocabulary that is familiar to the audience. Too much jargon can distract the audience while they try to understand new meanings and applications.
- ***Explain new or complex terms.*** When you use familiar words and phrases the audience will understand your content much more quickly. You can also introduce new vocabulary and give brief explanations with examples, as each one is introduced. In this way, you are extending the audience's knowledge and demonstrating your own knowledge to the tutor. You could decide to create a Glossary that provides brief descriptions of the terms used in your presentation. Give this to the audience with other handouts that you have created.
- ***Speak clearly.*** Speak a little slower than you do in everyday conversations with friends and colleagues. This will give the audience time to listen and understand what you are saying while getting used to your style of speech.
- ***Use an interesting tone of voice.*** If you sound interesting you will probably make the content interesting. Showing some enthusiasm for the topic can generate interest from the audience.
- ***Finish sentences.*** During communication with friends and colleagues we often do not need to finish sentences because they finish them for us or can make an accurate guess at the meanings without hearing everything spelt out. We may interrupt them or be interrupted ourselves. Generally, we get used to this style of communication and compensate for it by asking questions or for repetition of something we have not understood. In a presentation you will be expected to present the content using complete sentences. Whilst this may seem obvious, we have attended many events where speakers adopt an informal approach and pause before sentences are finished, leaving the audience guessing! This can be very irritating and exhausting to try to work out the correct meanings. Practise and rehearse completing your sentences and this will not be a problem for you.

For more discussion of these points read Chapter 3.

*2   **Visual communications***   We discuss this in more detail in Chapters 8 and 9. When you think about what makes presentations effective, it will be useful to consider how you can use images to communicate more effectively.

At this stage it will be useful to remember these principles:

- ***Use images to improve understanding.*** Sometimes, it is easier to use a picture instead of words to improve audience understanding. When you show a picture, you can ask them a question or suggest they think about the image in a certain way. You can then remain silent while they think about the image or the task you have set them. Images can also be used to direct audience attention away from you and onto the image on the screen. This may help to steady your nerves as it gives you a few seconds to perhaps take some deep breaths or check your notes.

- *Use images to save time.* If there is only a short amount of time you could include images as a quick way to cover some of the content. You have probably heard of the phrase, '*a picture paints a thousand words*' and this is very relevant to a student presentation.
- *Use images for interest.* Images use the visual sense whereas sound and speech use the auditory sense. Providing content in a variety of formats means that the audience has to use of a range of senses. This keeps them active in the process of receiving the presentation. We all have preferences and using a variety of communication approaches ensures a wider appeal to different members of the audience.
- *Use images for impact.* Images are more relevant for some topics than others but even if only a few can be included, they can be useful to create pauses and breaks in the delivery, generate discussion themes or make a lasting impression.

3   Non-verbal communications   You will also need to think about non-verbal communication, that is how you communicate using body language. There is a large amount of research in this area and you will probably not have the time to read about it while preparing your presentation. However, there are some key principles that you can use to improve your non-verbal communication during the presentation.

- *Choose whether to stand or sit.* In some situations such as in a seminar, you may be one of a group who sit in a circle or around a table. Check with the tutor what the best approach is. In many student presentations standing will be expected. Whether you sit or stand, you should try to convey some control and authority for your performance. This will be especially important for an interview presentation and a Viva.
- *Keep still.* Having agreed on the best position, try to keep still and stay in one place rather than moving around. Swaying backward and forward becomes distracting as does taking steps forward, backward or from side to side. For a group presentation, decide where each person will stand, who will move and when. Rehearse these changes to avoid collisions. The audience may laugh if this happens but you will probably not be amused!
- *Keep your hands still.* We all have a tendency to flap our hands while we speak. This is natural in most situations and while it might be used for enthusiasm, it can be a distraction during a presentation. If you do not use your hands to operate the technology or demonstrate something, hold cards or papers or clasp your hands lightly in front of you to reduce the waving around. Avoid all repetitive behaviours such as clasping and unclasping hands, folding your arms, using your pockets and shuffling your notes.

- *Face the audience as much as possible.* They will pick up non-verbal clues from your facial expression. This will also help you to 'sweep the group' by making brief eye contact with the audience. If you use PowerPoint do not turn to view the screen as your voice will become muffled. Use the image on the console or create paper images if you need them for memory purposes so that you do not need to turn to the screen. 'Sweeping' the audience frequently will help you to relax and may give you some feedback on what they find interesting or boring.

We discuss the use of body language in Chapter 3.

Appropriate use of technologies

In this chapter we use the term 'technologies' in a generic way. It could mean a medical aid such as a dummy in a first aid presentation, a specialist piece of equipment such as a sewing machine or food blender or the widely used Microsoft PowerPoint. In each of the examples given in Chapter 1 we list the type of technology that you would be expected to use in that situation.

Chapter 9 provides some detailed discussion on using PowerPoint. Here, we are interested in how using some technology improves the presentation to make it more effective. We suggest the following key principles:

1 In most situations, the technology should be 'the servant' not 'the master'. You should control it rather than letting it dominate the presentation. If it creates problems, it will distract the presenters and the audience from the content that needs to be delivered.
2 It needs to be fit for purpose. Use it as an integral part of the presentation rather than an add-on feature.
3 The technology should improve what you have to communicate so that the audience gains a better understanding of your content. However, it may be that the topic will not be improved by the software that has to be used.
4 Rehearse using the technology, especially if it is an essential part of demonstrating your skills in the presentation. You will need to feel confident in how you use it.
5 Have a backup system in case it fails. We have seen situations where the technology failed but the presentation was still effective because the presenter had made copies of notes and screen shots that he then worked through with the audience. If you have rehearsed your presentation well, this type of experience will be less of a problem.

Clear supporting documentation

As part of your presentation, you may have been asked to create handouts but even if handouts are not essential, the audience may find summaries, lists of key points, or a print out of the slides useful. Good handouts can be used in the future and may give a 'feel good factor' to the presentation. The style and level of detail given in this documentation should be relevant to the presentation situation and audience needs.

You will also need to think about how these documents will be used during the presentation. Will you give them out before the presentation so that the audience can use them to make their own notes, or will this approach distract their attention from the presenter or visuals on a screen? It is helpful at the start of the presentation to explain how you have decided to deal with the handouts and the level of note taking that will be needed by audience members. In some situations it may be more helpful and enjoyable to concentrate on the audio and visual content rather than trying to make notes for future recall. Supporting documentation is discussed in more detail in Chapter 8.

Suitable audience participation

Student presentations vary considerably as we discussed in Chapter 1. Some will be expected to involve the audience in activities or discussion at certain times within the presentation. Others will be more formal, having no interaction at all or requiring questions and answers only at the end of the presentation. Inevitably, the purpose of the presentation will influence the amount of audience participation but interesting participation can be a worthwhile experience for all concerned. Different perspectives on a topic can be identified and explored further. Creative ideas can stimulate discussion and extend understanding.

The briefing details for the presentation should explain the level of interaction expected and this will probably influence the design, level and structure of the content. In most situations, it is important for the presenter(s) to remain in control of the presentation and this includes managing the interactions with members of the audience. Make it clear at the start of the presentation how you expect them to participate by explaining how and when you want to take questions. There are several approaches to consider, for example, you could suggest that they can ask for further explanation if they do not understand a point you are covering but they must leave their general questions to the end of the presentation. This helps to set the ground rules and maintains a feeling of control for the presenters. It can sometimes be helpful to say how many minutes have been allocated for questions at the end of the presentation. If a member of the audience repeatedly tries to interrupt the flow, you can then remind them that there will be time for their questions at the end. Use this as a warning however. One or two students monopolizing this final stage of the presentation may irritate other members of the audience and cause them to withdraw from any further discussion.

If you want the audience to participate during the presentation, there are several techniques you can use to encourage this. You can do this by inviting questions or directly involving chosen members of the audience with tasks, exercises and demonstrations.

If the audience is very quiet and do not immediately pose questions when you ask for any, it can be useful to prepare a few of your own questions that you use to extend the topic and perhaps stimulate further questions. Some audience members may be more willing to answer an open or a direct question from you rather than raise their own question.

Finally, questions can seem tedious after the third or fourth so select them carefully and link the ones that are similar to avoid any repetition and retain the audience's interest. Answer questions succinctly then move on. If someone keeps going back to the same point, close the discussion and offer to discuss it with them when the presentation is over. We discuss understanding your audience in Chapter 6.

We began this chapter by reminding you of the usefulness of presentations in learning situations and acknowledging the diversity in how they are used. For presentations to be effective, they need to fulfil their aims and objectives, be enjoyable and offer developmental opportunities for the presenters and the audiences.

KEY PRINCIPLES FOR DELIVERING EFFECTIVE PRESENTATIONS

1 Plan and prepare well. Preparing a presentation usually takes longer than you think it will. Good time management is essential.
2 Develop relevant and interesting content. Make sure it is useful for the audience and is suitable for the purpose of the presentation.
3 Create a clear and logical structure that will be easy for the audience to understand and will help you to feel in control.
4 Communicate clearly using a variety of skills and techniques.
5 Use the technologies suitable for the purpose. They should enhance the delivery rather than control or restrict it.
6 Create clear supporting documentation that will be useful for the presenter and the audience during and after the presentation.
7 Think about how much audience participation you need and include this in your content and structure.
8 Finally, make sure that you understand the purpose of the presentation and how it will be assessed by the tutor and measured for quality and effectiveness by the audience.

The following chapters discuss all of these features in more detail.

3 Improving Individual Performance

LEARNING OBJECTIVES

Reading this chapter will help you to:

- rehearse key aspects of your presentation
- anticipate and deal with your presentation nerves
- use mental rehearsal techniques to go through the presentation in advance
- study other presenters
- improve your awareness of how your body contributes to a successful presentation
- become more confident through using your voice efficiently

We believe that you can greatly improve performance by including rehearsal in the stages of preparation. In our experience, students often spend time on the planning and some research but frequently deliver the presentation without much rehearsal. Even if the content is good, the overall impression of the presentation may only be average if there is insufficient rehearsal to reduce your stress.

We are going to discuss rehearsal under the following two main headings:

1 Improving the content.
2 Improving your individual performance.

1 Improving the content

Learn the factual content and structure of the presentation

Learn the factual content and structure of the presentation so that you gain a clear understanding of the topic. This will help you to feel more confident and should also help you to handle any interruptions more effectively. You do not have to know every single word of your presentation by heart, but you have to know the main points.

Rehearse speaking aloud

It can be helpful to hear the sound and emphasis of your voice. It usually takes longer to say something than to read it and the audience will need time to gain an understanding of what you are saying. Speaking the content out loud can help you to use pauses to slow down your delivery. Most people speak quicker than usual when they are nervous, and practising pauses should help to reduce your nerves. How you actually speak, the vocal delivery that you use to make your presentation effective, is a slightly different issue, and we are going to consider that later in this chapter.

Adjusting the content to fit the time

Where the presentation timing is preset, it is important that the pace of the verbal and image presentation are in a correct sequence. Rehearsal will help you to set realistic timing and adjust your pace of delivery to accommodate pauses and changes of voice tone for emphasis. You will then be able to edit the content, perhaps deciding what facts you need to discuss and what can be covered in the handouts or visual aids.

Rehearsal as part of a group

If you are taking part in a group presentation, you will need to rehearse together *as a team* to make sure that there is a balance between the parts and that suitable links are developed between individual members. There is usually a tendency to prepare far too much content for the time available. So you may need to edit what you have found by giving key points with examples during the presentation but more detail in the handouts. This should prevent the presentation overrunning and will allow for some interruptions or delayed starts. We discuss working for group presentations in more detail in Chapter 6.

Rehearse in the physical environment

If possible, try to rehearse in the actual room where the presentation will take place. If you can, check the layout of the room before the event and look at the type of furniture available to see how formal or informal the room will be.

Look at where the tables and chairs will be placed, how they are laid out and how far you will be standing from the audience. Check the height of the tables and the amount of space available to spread out your papers or cards.

Try to find out before the presentation whether you will be able to arrange the room and presentation area to suit your needs or whether you will have to accept the layout provided. (See also Chapter 10 on room layout.) With many student presentations, re-arranging the room may not be an option but it is usually worth considering as this can influence your style of delivery or how confident you feel.

Practise using your prompts

Speakers who have attended courses on public speaking often use cards with prompts during their presentations. However, although you may use this method, many students find it easier to use A4 sheets of paper for supplementary notes. For PowerPoint, use the notes option. If you want to use cards, use big ones!

Rehearse the use of technology

You will want to feel confident so that you are not distracted by the technology during the presentation. Think about where the cables will be placed and whether there will be a need to use a microphone. If you are on your own, you will also need to consider whether you will require additional help to operate the technology. If you are in a group, who is going to operate the technology? Deciding this can reduce distracting movements by the group members as they change places but timing the technology with the delivery may need extra rehearsal. Also it may help each speaker to feel more confident to operate the technology while they are speaking.

The presenter should aim to keep looking at their notes and the audience rather than at each slide as it appears on the screen. As they turn to look at this, their voice will be less audible and the behaviour becomes predictable and tedious to watch. It can be more effective to just do this occasionally especially where the slide contains more detailed and important information. It may then be helpful for the presenter to move to the side of the room and appear to share the position the audience is viewing, and reflect on the content of the slide. This is exactly the sort of movement that can be practised in advance. We discuss using the technology in more detail in Chapter 8.

2   Improving your individual performance

Developing your self-confidence when presenting

Many students feel highly nervous about undertaking class presentations, especially when there is a mark attached. This is very understandable. It is all very well for tutors to say things like 'Well, there is no pressure on you', 'You'll do fine on the day', or 'Don't worry, we will be doing it in quite an informal way'.

However, tutors have to stand up and present regularly each week. They are highly practised and usually fairly self-confident as a result. The first time you come to do a presentation, you will not have had a lot of practice. You may not feel very confident about the subject area, and you may not have all that much time to prepare. So no wonder you might well feel nervous; it's a very sensible reaction to have. But that doesn't mean that you will 'fail', or that you will do a poor presentation. It simply means that you are understandably nervous. This is an appropriate feeling. So you will be pleased to know that there are many different ways in which you can overcome your nerves, and go on to do an excellent presentation.

Now we are going to help you to develop individual techniques that will give you authority, a confident posture and a confident voice.

What are presentation nerves?

Imagine this scenario. You discover that in one of the modules in the new semester, you will be required to do a presentation to the class on a subject you do not know much about. This will count as 40 per cent of the overall mark. What are your reactions?

- Delighted?
- Appalled?
- Glad to accept the challenge?
- Already feeling terrified?
- Thinking of changing to another module?

The symptoms of presentation nerves   If you said yes to some of the above, you may already be feeling the beginnings of presentation nerves. Have you already suffered from nervousness before a presentation? Most people have, and the symptoms might include:

- sweaty palms
- shaky hands
- dry throat
- increased pulse rate
- twitching knees or legs
- forced and unnatural laughter
- tenseness, pain in the stomach
- extravagant and unnatural hand gestures
- the brain just switching off – you cannot function properly

What are your personal symptoms of stress?

We are programmed to have nervous reactions and to be tense in certain situations. Sometimes it is highly appropriate to be tense. In an emergency, you probably do not want to be totally calm, collected and relaxed! But much of the time, stress is not an appropriate reaction. Or rather, too much stress is not an appropriate reaction. Some stress is helpful. When you are preparing your presentation, and when you are undertaking it, it is important to feel a little bit nervous, to have some kind of edge on your performance. You need to feel energized, positive and ready to go. Do not worry about nerves, but read the next section to learn how to build up your confidence.

You can learn to build up your confidence

Your strongest single resource in developing presentation skills is your brain. But you can also use your body, your voice and your eyes to enhance the presentation and to boost your confidence.

Using your brain 1. Association and disassociation A key skill in any stressful situation is the ability to:

- be yourself and
- stand outside yourself

at the same time.

It is useful to know how to be able to move between being:

1 totally focused on your inner feelings and standing outside yourself and
2 able to look at what is happening around you from an objective perspective, without nerves, calm and objective

Some people do it naturally, and are not really aware that they are doing it. Some people very consciously use these techniques. These two places to be are sometimes called states of Association and Disassociation. See Table 3.1 (page 36).

In effect, when you develop an ability to stand outside yourself, you are acting. That's what actors do, they inhabit the body and the thought processes of someone else, for a short period of time. Some people are likely to be in this dissociated state for much of their professional life. If you do not cultivate a certain distance from pain and distress, you can get too close and get badly damaged.

Table 3.1 Association or disassociation

Association Seeing the world through your own eyes	☐ In the experience ☐ Be here now ☐ In touch with what is happening ☐ Aware of own feelings ☐ Not really aware of time ☐ Seeing things with your own eyes ☐ Example – on holiday, with a loved one; any time that you want to be yourself!
Disassociation Putting yourself at a distance; seeing yourself performing or going through actions	☐ Slightly distant ☐ Remote ☐ On the sidelines ☐ Watching yourself performing ☐ Very aware of time ☐ Able to stand outside yourself ☐ Example – an examination, difficult meeting, being criticized

It is one way of successfully undertaking a presentation. You *become* the successful presenter. You do not have to stay like that afterwards, but for the period of the presentation, you have a special role to play.

This concept of association and disassociation can be used to practise for meetings, interviews etc. and for any experience that you might find challenging. It is linked to the technique of mental rehearsal, mentally practising the event over and over again.

Mental rehearsal You cannot actually do your presentation in front of an audience more than once. But in your head, you can practise many times. This approach is used by many top sports stars.

The following exercise combines both *association and disassociation* and *mental rehearsal*.

1 Imagine yourself undertaking a successful presentation.
2 Describe to yourself the performance that you are going to do. As you describe what is going to happen, you look at a picture of yourself, and hear yourself running through the presentation, standing in front of the group. Be absolutely clear about what is happening and see all the details. You are looking at somebody very much like you, and they are successfully carrying out the presentation.

3   The person you are watching is doing an effective and successful presentation. Notice the way that the audience is reacting; notice the confident posture of the speaker and how they engage with the group in front of them.

4   It is as though you are watching yourself undertaking a presentation and just seeing what happens. You observe yourself, coolly and objectively. If you want to, imagine sitting in a corner of the room in which the presentation occurs or yourself at the back of the room, watching somebody like yourself do the presentation. The point is that the you at the back of the room is separated out, disassociated, from the you at the front, successfully presenting to a group.

You might want to do this several times over. Be very clear about what is happening and what could be done to improve it. Focus on all the details including what the presenter is wearing, colours around the presenter in the room, what people are saying to the presenter, the atmosphere in the room. If for any reason, you just cannot imagine yourself doing this, fine. Who could you imagine doing it? A friend? Relative? Some celebrity? A television personality? Just imagine what it would be like if they were doing the presentation for you.

5   When you have run through your observation of the presenter and the successful presentation several times, just relax. Switch off for a couple of minutes.

6   Now become yourself. Visualize yourself actually doing the successful presentation. When you are ready, and only when you are ready, you then 'become yourself' and imagine doing the presentation from your own perspective. Step into your own shoes, looking out through your eyes at the audience. As you mentally rehearse, you see what you will be seeing in that situation, feeling the movements and expressions of your body, and hearing what your voice will sound like, and watching the reaction of your audience in front of you.

You are totally in your own body, doing the presentation really well and effectively. Make what you see happening in front of you as real as possible. Be very aware of colours around you, your voice tones, the reactions of the audience, as you begin to create a mood of successfully completing the presentation. What sounds will you be able to hear? What will the feelings both of tension and excitement be like? In which part of your body will you feel them? Imagining yourself dealing with questions, issues and problems with complete confidence and style!

7   Now have a quick break for one minute. Come back to the present. Do something else and distract yourself for a few seconds; for instance, count down from 100 to 40.

8   How did it go? You then ask yourself how the presentation went. You might want to be particularly aware of feelings of being comfortable or uncomfortable, tense or more relaxed, as you went through the presentation.

9   Make changes. If you need to make changes to the way you imagine the performance going, you might want to imagine yourself making a presentation as above, from Stage 1 onwards.

10   In conclusion. Continue to go through stages 1–9 until you feel really confident that you can do a superb job. When you have rehearsed it in your head several times, the actual event will feel much less scary, because you will have been there already.

These techniques of mental rehearsal are already backed up by studies in the literature on sports people and on medical patients. There is considerable evidence that mental rehearsal and visualizing your presentation will greatly improve your performance on the day.

Using your brain 2. Thinking about excellent presenters   Do you know somebody whom you consider to be an excellent presenter? A tutor, a friend or a television presenter? What is it that makes them good at what they do? Make time to observe them. Look out for such characteristics as:

- body movements
- gestures
- eye contact
- voice tone and pace
- their powers of persuasion
- the kinds of language they use

Write down the points which you feel make the person a good presenter. Decide which of these you feel you are comfortable with. Use a friend to give you some feedback. It is quite likely that not all of your role model's skills will work for you. But some of them certainly will do. You will be able to tell which ones you feel comfortable with and which can, therefore, serve to increase your feelings of confidence.

Using your brain 3. Have a powerful memory to boost your confidence   You will almost certainly have a positive feeling that you can take with you when you begin your presentation. This might be:

- an internal image of a presenter that you enjoy
- a photograph of someone you like or admire
- the sound of your voice when you made a previous successful presentation
- a particular piece of music
- a phrase that sums up your positive feelings such as 'I'm a winner', 'This is going to work', or 'I WILL succeed'

If you have had success of any kind in your life, you can take the feelings associated with that success with you when you do your presentation. All you need to do is practise recalling the feeling, the memory, and the image in advance and lock them in position. Practice makes perfect. So start practising remembering positive feelings of success rather than feelings of failure, as so many people do when they think about presentations.

If you want a very quick and simple alternative, try associating a positive confident feeling with a smell such as peppermint or lemon aroma therapy oil on a tissue. Practise associating that peppermint smell with feeling confident. Before you start your presentation, simply have a quick sniff of peppermint oil, and feel the confidence beginning to flow through you. (Make sure it is a clean confident smell, not a gentle sleepy smell such as lavender!)

Using your body confidently

Audiences and tutors make initial judgments about presenters on appearance and body language, even before they start listening to what you say. To build up good rapport with an audience and thus attract their attention and interest, you can help yourself by developing effective body language skills.

The following sections offer some guidelines on body language. There are two things that you can do to improve the way you use your body when you present:

1 practise the techniques below
2 observe professional presenters, such as those on television, paying attention to the way in which they use their hands and their eyes

Use a video camera If you have access to the technology, ask a friend to help you with a video camera. It can be useful to get some more sense of how others will see you. But do not allow the technology to distract you from how you look and move. Do not be discouraged if you appear different or sound different from the way you hoped to be.

How you look: your clothes You should ensure that what you wear is both comfortable and suitable for the occasion. You need to feel relaxed; you also need to present an appropriate image to your audience. So what is appropriate? For a very low profile presentation, you might do fine with your normal jeans, trainers and top, for instance. But if you are looking for marks and it is a more serious presentation, you will almost certainly want to dress slightly more formally.

You may have noticed that some professional presenters like to wear something highly coloured or bright, so that they stand out. But you will probably not want to allow what you wear to get in the way of what you are saying. You might want to consider a colourful shirt for a man, a bright top or a scarf for a woman. The clothes need to be simple and smart, so that you look appropriately dressed, comfortable and relaxed.

How you look: the way you stand   You can do something very useful for weeks before the presentation takes place – practise how you stand. Try this:

- your feet are apart, approximately in line with your hips, and your feet are slightly turned out
- your feet are relaxed and you can feel the ground underneath them
- you have made sure that your knees are relaxed, not locked; you can easily bend them
- your hands are relaxed and so are your arms, hanging loosely by your sides
- you are standing upright and your spine feels straight
- your neck is straight and your head is directly above your neck. In other words, you are not leaning forward nor leaning back. Your head is so positioned that you can imagine a golden cord passing up through your spine through your neck and up through your head. The golden cord carries on up pulling gently, so that your head, your neck and your spine are all in a direct line with each other. (In fact, your head is actually quite heavy, something like 4.25 kg or 9 pounds. If the head is not in line with your neck, the neck can get quite uncomfortable.)

In this open and relaxed posture, you will be able to breathe deeply and your voice will be clear and strong. Try to avoid crossing your arms on your chest, hunching your shoulders and crossing one leg in front of the other. Similarly do not lean forward, slumping onto the lectern or table, if there is one. These kinds of behaviour are all obvious signs of tension and they will not help you.

How you look: your movement   A completely still presenter will soon tire the audience and a presenter who moves continually will distract from the words and be difficult for the audience to follow. You will want to move carefully and effectively, emphasizing points, helping your audience to relax and keeping them engaged.

It is okay to move but do not overdo it. It is better to move slightly than to keep completely still, like a frozen statue. A mirror; or even better a video camera, can be incredibly helpful for looking at yourself and examining your movements. Avoid rocking back and forward as some nervous presenters do.

Try rehearsing in front of a mirror or at a table, to get used to handling notes or cards, and check how much you use your hands. Whilst this can be useful for emphasis, it can also be distracting, so try to keep hand waving to a minimum. Using a mirror is a technique used by many actors and professional communicators and can improve your performance considerably.

Gestures   Using your hands can help in the same way that whole body movements can: to relax, stimulate and illustrate. If you find it hard to use your hands naturally, then the best policy is to hold them by your sides. Try not to:

- clasp hands behind the back. This looks much too formal.
- fold them in front. This is usually interpreted as a very defensive posture.
- keep them stuck in your pockets throughout the presentation. This can look either casual or nervous.
- scratch, poke or stroke yourself. As you have probably observed, this is quite a common nervous reaction amongst stressed presenters.
- wring your hands together. This can look dishonest or slightly peculiar.
- fiddle with keys, pens, pencils, coins, lucky charms, worry beads, etc. You will just look nervous.

If you enjoy using your hands, make them part of the presentation. Practise using your hands to make key points and to illustrate ideas. However the main issue with using your hands is to be natural.

Eye contact   Eyes are one of your best tools for involving the audience in what you are saying. Good posture, movement and gestures will be of little use if you fail to support them with appropriate eye contact. If you are an inexperienced presenter, you might find it very difficult to look any member of the audience in the eye. A useful technique is to try to focus between and slightly above the eyes; the audience will feel that they are being looked at and involved, unless you are extremely close. The size of the audience will determine the appropriate level of eye contact but here are two important guidelines to follow, regardless of audience size.

1 Never hold one person's gaze for more than five seconds maximum.
2 Never appear to be 'watching tennis', swinging your eyes (and head) from one side of the audience to the other.

For presentation to small groups, fewer than about six people, focus on individuals in turn.

For medium-sized audiences pick out individuals at random, drawing them into the presentation. Take them from different parts of the room in turn. With a class of about 20 people, there would probably be enough time to look at every individual but please do not do this by moving from one to the next in order of their seating arrangement! Do it randomly. Eye contact can also be used to 'pull back' any individual who appears to be distracted or bored, if you are feeling sufficiently confident.

In a medium-size or large group, if you look at one individual, several other people around that individual will also feel that you have looked at them. You can impact on five people just by focusing briefly on one of them.

With a big group, a presenter will probably be unable to focus on individuals. In this case, choose small areas of the audience at a time, looking either at the group or at one individual in the centre of the group. In this way, all of the audience can be involved. There is more on audiences in Chapter 6.

Using your voice   Using your voice is a very specialist area. It is amazing that although we are all taught to speak, we are not taught to use our voice. Unless we become actors, singers or other kinds of voice professionals, or unless we damage our voices in some way, most of us will never receive voice training. What happens to most people's voices when stressed by a presentation? The voice can:

- speed up
- become higher
- become flat and monotonous
- become nervous and you start to stutter – if you have a hint of a stutter, that stutter may become worse
- become smaller – you may find it very difficult to project your voice
- display lack of clarity, so that you are constantly having to clear your throat
- become 'croaky' or harsh – the nervousness and tension cause the vocal cords to dry up
- become BIGGER – too loud and overconfident

So what can we do to prevent our voice deserting us when we are under pressure?

First of all, let us learn a little bit about how the voice works. Then we are going to suggest key activities that you can do to improve the quality of your voice for presentations.

There are three aspects to the voice – the lungs which generate the air, the vocal cords which vibrate, and the mouth, nose, palate, and so on which shape the sound.

Breathing   The voice starts with breathing, and that means starting with a relaxed body. If you have a relaxed torso, you will be able to breathe properly. But if your stomach and ribs are tight and tense, you will simply not be able to draw in adequate breath to push up towards the voice box or larynx.

Everyone instinctively knows that if you want to talk loudly, you have to take a deep breath. To be able to speak effectively in a pressured situation, we need to be able to take a deep breath and then take extra breaths as we talk, to keep the voice at an appropriate level. So adequate breathing is absolutely essential.

Start by relaxing your body. You might want to try this lying down in a relaxed position on your back, or you might want to do it standing, because that's probably the position you will be in when you are presenting!

Breathing through your nose and out through your mouth. Think about any physical tension that there might be – your feet, your ankles, your legs, your stomach, your back, your chest, your throat, your shoulders, each arm, your hands, and then back up towards your face and then up to the top of your head. All the time, keep breathing, and allow the air to flow in and out through your relaxed mouth.

When you start your presentation, you will want to feel relaxed and strong, safe in the knowledge that the breath can flow through you from the bottom of your lungs up to, and through, your voice box, the larynx.

Start today to become more and more aware of your breathing. When you come to present, you will continually be aware of your breathing right through the presentation. So you will be able to check your breathing and start to take a deep breath from time to time. Make your breathing strong and deep.

Your posture   The way that you stand will have a huge impact on the way that you breathe. The way that you breathe will have a huge impact on how you sound. Think about whether you will be sitting or standing during the presentation and which will be most appropriate for the event. Will you need to move around the room or be expected to remain in one place?

Are you comfortable standing in one place? Some people are, and some people find that in order to express themselves, they have to move during a presentation. Avoid standing frozen like a statue, try not to pace about like a caged animal, but aim to move naturally and appropriately.

Whether you need to move around or remain still, it is vital to get your posture right, so that your voice box is relaxed. Follow our tips; stand tall, with your weight equally distributed, in a straight line and with relaxed knees. If you can learn to stand in a strong upright and relaxed stance, you will feel much better and your voice will be stronger too. If you want to learn more about your posture, you might consider either Tai Chi or the Alexander Technique. Your local public library should have books on both of these.

Your voice tone and pitch   Your tone is the sound you make. Everyone has an individual sound. It comes from the breath resonating in your chest, your skull and your mouth itself. The mouth is the most important contributor to tone because it can alter the sounds so dramatically. You can become more aware of tone by humming. Practise making your humming a little lighter and higher, or a little darker and stronger.

Pitch means the musical quality of your voice. Ideally you should be able to vary the pitch, but not be constantly swooping up and down in an irritating 'singsong' fashion. Your voice needs to be lubricated, and more specifically, the 'vocal cords' which vibrate need to be lubricated. So drink some water before the presentation and during it, have a glass of water with you when you are talking. Pitch is created by the vibration of the vocal cords. The vocal cords can only vibrate fully if the throat is relaxed. That means that you must do everything in your power to keep your throat relaxed. For instance, a tight collar can greatly restrict your throat and therefore affect your pitch. You will find a lot more about the more sophisticated aspects of voice production for presentations in McCarthy and Hatcher (2002).

Tips on using your voice   Here are 12 different ways to prepare your voice for the presentation:

1   Practise. Try to get access to a tape recorder, video player, an MP3 player or some other form of recording device, so that you can listen to the sound of your voice. Even if it does not sound as good as you would wish, the recording will give you an impression of your voice. How does it normally sound? How would you like it to sound for the presentation?
2   Warm up the voice. Warm your voice up before you start speaking. Your vocal muscles, your larynx, need to be warmed up just like any other muscles. Drink some water before you start and then undertake a simple exercise such as repeating nonsense rhymes: 'Ding dong bing bong' – up and down the scales; or tongue-twisters such as: 'Susie sells sea shells on the sea shore'. It is perfectly okay to just speak nonsense, providing that you are using lots of different sounds, at different levels, and going up and down the scale. You might find it helpful to actually say some of the key phrases from your presentation. Try saying them in different ways. But focus on warming up the voice.

3   Do not fade away. Watch out for fading away at the end of sentences. This is normally associated with nervousness or lack of confidence. Practise in normal speech, with your friends. Aim to finish the sentence clearly and strongly. This is especially true of the last part of your presentation.

4   Keep breathing. Practise taking several deep breaths from the bottom of the lungs before you start speaking AND continue to take breaths throughout your presentation. Some people simply forget to breathe during their presentation!

5   Ensure that your neck is comfortable. If your neck feels stiff, gently relax it. You may want to search out a book on specific neck exercises. If not, gently rub your neck with your hands to warm it. Stand tall; allow your spine and neck to lengthen slightly. Relax your shoulder blades and then roll them forwards. Stand tall again.

6   Learn to yawn more often. Learn to relax the jaws before the presentation by moving them around and by deliberately yawning to keep the jaws relaxed. However, it is probably a bad move to yawn during the presentation, unless you want your audience to fall asleep!

7   Practise smiling. You can relax the facial muscles by smiling. Not only will a smile to your audience relax your face but it will of course also relax your audience. While you are preparing, you will find that a few smiles will relax you during the presentation, and an encouraging smile to the audience will help them relax too.

8   Practise your pace. Practise emphasizing keywords, practise going through key elements of the presentation, ensuring that you go at the right speed, not too fast nor too slow. You do not have to always start at the beginning. Keep it fresh by practising just some parts, or starting near the end.

9   Practise your tone and pitch. Consider learning more about your voice and how it works.

10   Be prepared for pauses. Pauses, given at key points in the presentation are also useful for the audience to reflect on the content or a question that you have posed. Rehearsal will help you to be more relaxed about providing these pauses and stop you rushing to fill any silences. Pauses may also provide opportunities for members of the audience to murmur in agreement or make a brief comment to another colleague.

11   Emphasis. Learn to emphasize key phrases during the presentation. You can use both pauses and emphasis to clarify certain points, and to repeat key messages.

12   Learn from experience. Always be prepared to learn from every lecture, every presentation that you attend. Keep learning.

Conclusion

Making sure that the presentation is well rehearsed will improve both your performance and enjoyment of the event. It will help to reduce your nerves and increase your confidence on the day. Rehearsal will also help to improve your understanding of the content and enable you to answer questions more competently. Practice does not necessarily make perfect, but practice certainly makes sure that you will deliver confidently and powerfully.

KEY PRINCIPLES FOR DOING YOUR VERY BEST INDIVIDUAL PERFORMANCE

1 Presentation skills are learned skills – and practice makes perfect.
2 Understand your presentation nerves.
3 Take a powerful image with you into the presentation.
4 Practise how you will stand and move.
5 Learn to use your voice.
6 Practise your breathing.

Further reading

McCarthy, P. and Hatcher, C. (2002) *Presentation Skills: The Essential Guide for Students*. London: Sage.

4 Presenting as Part of a Group

LEARNING OBJECTIVES

Reading this chapter will help you to:

- recognize the benefits of group presentations
- understand how problems can develop in group working
- identify strategies for reducing group problems
- work effectively to deliver a group presentation

This is a long chapter which is divided into the following sections:

The context for group work
Benefits of working for group presentations
Problems of working for group presentations
Techniques for effective group work
Key principles

The context for group work

Group presentations are used frequently in academic courses. These presentations usually involve covering some content from your modules but they also provide opportunities for developing team working and project management skills as preparation for employment.

Much of the advice given throughout this book is relevant to group as well as individual presentations but in this chapter we concentrate on the special nature of group presentations. We discuss how to work together as a team so that your presentations are interesting and effective.

Although we prefer to concentrate on the positive features of group presentations, in our experience they can be very stressful for everyone involved. They can sometimes demoralize and demotivate students, rather than help to improve their presentation skills. Negative experiences of being let down by team members or feelings of a lack of control, anger and frustration tend to stay with us long after the event is over. When students complain to tutors about having to work with less committed students, tutors usually suggest that the experience is seen as a useful preparation for the workplace where you cannot usually choose your work colleagues. Therefore, you have to learn to work alongside or with them as part of several team situations.

If you are aware of the potential problems of group work then you will be better prepared to deal with them. You will understand how these problems happen and perhaps be able to reduce them, or at least be able to resolve them so that the presentation can be delivered to a reasonable standard. Over time, this will help you to become an effective team player, not only for presentations, but for other work situations. Being part of a successful group event can be an exhilarating experience.

As an employee you will almost certainly experience working in teams where your individual effort contributes to a team or project situation. Many organizations provide staff training to improve individual performance in teams. However, in organizations, the group will probably be managed in some way such as through a reporting committee, Project Manager or Supervisor. There may be reasonable levels of resources and time given to work on the different tasks needed. For student group presentations you may be given a briefing sheet and just told to get on with it! This approach often causes problems because group presentations usually need more careful management than is available.

There is a large amount of research into the benefits and problems of working in groups and teams and into the features that make them effective in both social situations and in the working environment. We discuss briefly some of the published research that we think you will find useful.

We have also carried out our own research into what makes effective group presentations and our results produced similar evidence to the established advantages and disadvantages of team working. Over a period of three years, we asked several cohorts of students to list what they thought were the benefits and problems of group presentations. We then asked them to suggest techniques they had developed to work well as a group and to think about what they had learned from group presentations. Finally, we asked if they had a preference for group or individual presentations. It was interesting that although they thought working for group presentations was often stressful, a majority of our students preferred group rather than individual presentations. We have included their responses in the following sections on the benefits and problems of working in groups.

Benefits of working for group presentations

We discussed the benefits of student presentations in Chapter 1 and these all apply in some way to group presentations. However, our students identified some specific benefits for working in groups and we outline these below under the following headings:

Teamwork can be motivating
Wider range of skills and knowledge available
Group performance can be higher than individual performance
Group work offers social opportunities
The group event can be more enjoyable than an individual performance

Teamwork can be motivating

For group presentations, group motivation may be higher than for working individually. The dynamics of the team can encourage you to be accountable and deliver what is expected for your contribution. You may feel reluctant to let other team members down and this can increase your commitment to delivering a good presentation rather than just seeing it as another assignment. Your workload may not be as large as for an individual event and the work may be completed in a shorter amount of time. This can be useful if you have little free time outside of formal lectures or classes.

Wider range of skills and knowledge available

A wider range of skills and knowledge is available in a group than from one individual and members can contribute what they are best at and learn new skills from the other members. This can encourage you to aim for higher levels of achievement. However, you will also have to learn to compromise and listen to others in the group. This is useful for problem solving where different ideas can be suggested and adapted so that the presentation content is richer and more interesting than if you were working on your own. Working on group presentations can offer good opportunities for peer learning.

Group performance can be higher than individual performance

If assessed, the final mark for the group may be higher than an individual member could earn. Of course this can work the other way but many of our students believed that group presentations raised their individual performance to a higher level than when they worked alone. They suggested this was partly due to increased motivation but also because group presentations offer opportunities to rehearse in front of others which improves your own contribution and performance. This also helps to increase your confidence. Whilst you can be criticized in these rehearsals, this criticism can sometimes be easier to take from another group member than from outsiders such as tutors or members of the audience. This shared experience gives everyone in the group opportunities for improvement.

Group work offers social opportunities

The social element of group presentations can be useful for making new friends. You will probably have to work with people in your cohort who you have not spoken to before. You may need to hold several meetings to plan, prepare and then rehearse the presentation. These meetings can be a combination of work and social time. They help you to network with other students.

The group event can be more enjoyable than an individual presentation

Sharing the responsibility for the actual event gives mutual support because you all share the stress and tensions on the day. Group events can generate a sense of belonging and you may prefer them because you will probably speak for a shorter amount of time. Many students claim to be more confident when presenting in a group. They gain support from the other members and feel more relaxed and less intimidated than when presenting alone where all of the audience's attention is focused on them. As well as sharing the stress, the practical tasks can also be shared such as turning over slides, using the technology or welcoming the audience.

Finally, our students reported that watching group presentations was usually more interesting than watching presentations of individual students. Whilst this was sometimes because the content was more interesting, they also said the variety of speakers seemed to give these presentations a sense of energy and entertainment.

Problems of working for group presentations

Our students also described some problems of working in groups and several of these were similar to problems identified through wider research into the problems experienced in groups and teams. We think you will find it useful to read the brief summaries outlined below and reflect on how relevant they are to your own group presentations. Being aware of and understanding these problems may help you to deal with them if they arise or perhaps even help to prevent them from happening. Many of these problems overlap and are the natural consequences of people working together in groups, communities and societies but we discuss them in the context of student groups under the following headings:

- Individual behaviour and loss of control
- Different levels of commitment in the group
- Difficult group dynamics
- Size of the group
- Limited development of ideas
- Poor decision making
- The final group presentation seems fragmented

Problem: Individual behaviour and loss of control

This problem can be experienced in several different ways.

Some people prefer to work on their own, finding teamwork restrictive and limiting. They willingly take responsibility for aspects of their own lives but in group situations they leave the work to others. This may be because they do not like to share the event or performance with others. Alternatively, they may have not developed good interpersonal skills when working with others, especially their peers.

Some students are shy or anxious and feel embarrassed when working in groups. They may have a fear of looking stupid, lack confidence for speaking in the group meetings and feel some concern about having to rely on others for the work, or for being let down by another group member. Alternatively, they may also feel worried about letting down other members because they believe their own work is not of a high enough standard.

Loss of individual control over the final style and content of the presentation can also be a consequence of group work. It can be difficult having to compromise on the range of ideas suggested. You can sometimes feel that the final product is very different from what you would have developed alone, or if you were working in a different student group. Peer pressure may result in you doing a subject you would not have chosen and you see the whole thing as an unhappy experience.

Another similar problem can be that in group work, matching individual strengths to the work that needs doing can be difficult and you may end up responsible for tasks that you find difficult to complete while other group members are responsible for tasks that you would prefer. However, you could use this as an opportunity for your own development. Working under these pressures will almost certainly improve your team working and presentation skills.

Problem: Different levels of commitment in the group

One of the most frequent problems in group working is that not everyone puts the same amount of effort into the task. Group members may have a different work ethic or standards for the quality of their work and this will probably result in different levels of commitment to prepare for the group presentation. Being late or failing to turn up to meetings, for whatever reasons, causes stress to those who do attend, especially if the absent member is contributing a large proportion of the content. Whilst different levels of commitment to the task could be partly influenced by individual workloads there are wider factors such as individual attitudes to study.

Another aspect of the same problem however, is where one member chooses to do more work than the others. An over eager member can be irritating to the other members who then reduce their commitment to the presentation leaving the over eager member to get on with most of the work. By taking on more than their fair share, they may eventually come to feel resentful with their increased workload, even if they volunteered for extra tasks. This will change the group dynamics and perhaps cause factions within the group as we discuss in the next problem.

We all have a different pace of working and some of us are better than others at meeting deadlines and delivering work. Whilst this is one of the important skills we can learn from team working, student group presentations can be unpleasant and difficult while these skills are developed.

Problem: Difficult group dynamics

Group dynamics play a major role in the success or ineffectiveness of the group. Personality clashes between group members are common problems identified by students. Individual personalities can be the cause of problems when overpowering leaders can have too much influence on the final presentation, or with members, who procrastinate yet do not complete what they are responsible for.

Difficult people are usually difficult in many areas of their lives and you will probably not be able to change them while working together in a student group. In these situations it can be difficult to criticize their efforts even when the criticism is deserved. Perhaps the best way for you to deal with this is to adapt your own behaviour and contribution to make sure that the presentation is completed. Reflect on how some of the bad experience could have been prevented then avoid working with this person in the future, if this is possible!

Problem: Size of the group

The size of the group will also have an influence on the dynamics but this may have been decided by the tutor. If the group is too large to work well together individual efforts may be difficult to recognize or will be lost in the total contributions from all the group members. However, large groups are useful for prestigious events where a wide range of skills and contacts is needed. Smaller groups of three or four can be more effective in situations where all contributions are visible, accountable and essential for the final event. This is especially important when the presentation is assessed.

The size of the group sometimes influences communication issues; however, with the increasing use of e-mail, this is much less of a problem. Poor communication between group members can lead to misunderstandings about individual roles or responsibilities. Misunderstandings can lead to a risk of duplicating the content and effort of the work or feeling unsure of how much information is required to include in the content. This is more likely to happen when members have not worked together before or have never spoken to each other before they are allocated to a group. Setting up clear communication channels is essential for group work and will help to reduce this problem.

Problem: Limited development of ideas

It is easy to assume that ideas generated by 'brainstorming' in groups would be better than those developed by individuals. This is not always true however, and there is a lot of research evidence to show that the best ideas can be produced when individuals work alone and then share their ideas in a group session (Diehl and Stroebe, 1987).

Group ideas sessions need to be managed carefully so that each member has the chance to explain their ideas and explore the feasibility of these ideas with the group. One of the problems in 'brainstorming' sessions is that something called the *production-blocking effect* occurs. When members are speaking, others are not able to put their own ideas forward without interrupting. They may not be listening because they are holding their own ideas in their memories and waiting for a chance to speak. This impairs their thinking processes and their ability to generate more ideas. They may feel inhibited from both offering ideas aloud and from thinking of new ideas by the competing noise of other group members.

Problem: Poor decision making

Research by Rogelberg et al. (1992) found that while groups could be expected to make better decisions than individuals working alone, they constantly fell short of the quality of decisions made by their most capable individual members. This challenges the general belief that groups and teams produce better results than individuals.

There are several possible reasons for this. The process of '*Satisficing*' can happen whereby decisions are chosen that are immediately acceptable to the group. The first acceptable idea is identified and agreed on. Group members then spend time looking for reasons to justify their idea and reject other possible and sometimes better solutions (Cyert and March, 1963).

Another phenomenon of group decision making is known as '*Groupthink*' where the group almost become too cohesive in their choice of ideas (Janis, 1982, 1989). Groupthink can occur when decisions need to be made during workshops, committees, meetings and conferences. It generally occurs when several characteristics are present that include:

- the group is tightly bonded and is more concerned with their own cohesiveness than the quality of their work and decision making
- the group insulates itself from external opinions and information, especially when it is different from their own
- group members tend to choose the first available consensus option rather than systematically searching through all available options to choose the most appropriate (see satisficing above)
- there is pressure on the group to make a decision
- members may be dominated by one individual who pressures them to conform to the majority view

All of these characteristics can be present in student groups. They can happen when student groups have already worked together quite well and where the end result was of a reasonable quality and perhaps earned a good mark.

A third influence on group decision making is known as '*Risky Shift*' or '*Group Polarization*' where there is a tendency for groups to make more extreme decisions than the average of the individual members' decisions (Myers and Lamm, 1976). These decisions may be either more risky or more conservative, especially when the group is working under pressure. This is because individual members compare their ideas and opinions with those of the other group members, then move their opinions closer to these members rather than retaining their individual integrity. Some of our students have experienced this and say that it makes them angry with the other group members for how the presentation has turned out. They also feel angry with themselves for letting it happen.

Problem: The final group presentation seems fragmented

Sometimes, group presentations seem disjointed and are spoilt by how the individual members deliver their part of the presentation. The presentation needs to be cohesive, rather than delivered as a collection of separate parts. Individuals can rehearse their contribution alone so that when they come together, the links can be improved and the individual contributions reviewed and edited so that the final presentation can be delivered in the time allocated to the group.

Rehearsals are also important because this is when weak members can be identified, either for their lack of understanding or for their poorer presentation skills. This is the time to improve both individual and group performance so that the final event is as effective as possible.

Contingency plans can be made for any non-attendance of members and although you may hope it will not happen, you are less likely to feel let down by other members and more likely to perform as a cohesive group if you have arranged several rehearsals. This is especially important when a presentation is assessed and you all share the same mark.

Explaining the detail of these group processes is beyond the scope of this book and you do not need to have a full understanding of them to prevent them from happening in your group work. We all experience some of these processes in different areas of our working lives, even in family and friendship groups. The reason why we include these problems of group working is so that you will be aware of them as possible consequences of working with other students. Our students have found them useful for understanding some group events they have experienced. If you are aware of how some of these problems occur, then you can try to reduce the effect in the group by using some of the techniques that we offer below for effective group work. These have also emerged from the research and have been effective in a wide range of group and team situations.

Techniques for effective group work

There are many influences on how well a group works together and a range of techniques you can use to avoid or reduce some of the problems discussed above. We have chosen several that will help you in your group work and discuss them briefly under the following headings:

- Create physical and virtual environments
- Understand the stages of group development
- Consider the composition of the group
- Assign roles and responsibilities within the group
- Create a listening and decision-making culture
- Set clear group and individual goals
- Make individual performance visible to the group
- Deal with conflict or failure constructively

Create physical and virtual environments

In most student working situations, there will be little control over the physical working environment but it can be useful to recognize that the physical space can encourage productive work. You may be able to book rooms in your department or in the library if they have areas for group work. Tables and chairs set out in a square or circle can encourage good discussion. Flipcharts or whiteboards can be useful for recording key points in the discussion or final decisions. Perhaps the most important point here is that having an agreed meeting space can encourage attendance at meetings, generate discussion and encourage commitment to the presentation.

Increasingly, virtual environments are playing a part in supporting group work. If students travel long distances and live many miles apart, a virtual discussion space can be used to share ideas and report progress. Again, the main value is to emphasize the need to share ideas, knowledge and progress for the presentation.

Understand the stages of group development

How long a group has existed, the history and shared experience can influence how well you work together. Early in your course you will probably be working with people that you have not met before so the stages of group development are very important. You will need to spend some time getting to know the other members so that you understand how they work and communicate with each other. In this situation, it will probably take some time before you begin to work well as a cohesive group.

If you work with the same group on several presentations, the group dynamics will change as you get to know each other and gain experience of working together. During this time, the group norms develop so an experienced group will probably be more effective at an earlier stage than if you are working with strangers.

Research by Tuckman and Jensen (1977) identified five key stages of development that apply to many group situations regardless of the projects or tasks to be completed. We outline these below and use preparing a presentation as the example for each stage.

1 **Forming**. This stage is when you first meet to find out about the presentation and what you need to do to complete the assignment. Time is spent getting to know the other members and the skills and experience that they bring to the project. This shared awareness can help the group to identify the different roles for each group member including a group leader or facilitator. We discuss the group roles later in this chapter. During this stage, each member may begin to research the presentation topic so that you can contribute ideas during the next meeting.

2 **Storming**. This can be the stage where ideas are discussed and developed. However, also at this stage, conflict and arguments can develop through resistance to ideas and emotional interactions between different personalities in the group. Some members may try to change the decisions and direction of the group to suit their own needs. Dominant members may become assertive whereas the quieter, more reflective members may cope with any conflict by withdrawing to the margins of the group. If you have previously worked as a group this stage may be briefer than if you are strangers.

3 **Norming**. Conflicts are resolved through some negotiation and compromise and members begin to share ideas in a more productive way. The group norms develop for what are acceptable social and work behaviours for individual members. These can be agreed through direct discussion or they can evolve through more subtle means of approval and disapproval but once these are established, there are strong pressures on members to conform. Some of our students reported that this is the stage when they begin to enjoy working together. The 'invisible boundaries' are set out and they feel more certain of what is expected of them. Groups who have worked together before usually reach this stage much earlier in preparing their presentation than a group of strangers and this may be the reason why the tutor tells you to choose who you work with so that it saves you some valuable preparation time.

4 **Performing**. This is the stage where members are working well together as a team. They are adaptable and flexible in their attitude towards each other and to the tasks that are needed to create content or products for the presentation. By this stage members will be more confident to comment on the contributions of others and suggestions for edits will be given and received in a constructive way. We would expect this stage to also include delivering the presentation so that it will appear as a cohesive event rather than a collection of individual parts.

5 **Adjourning**. This is where the group disperses after completing the presentation but some closure is needed to mark the completion of the task. You may want to arrange a meeting to debrief and reflect on the successful features of the event or to discuss parts of the presentation which could have been improved. This will be especially useful if you are likely to be working with some of the same students on future presentations and want to improve your overall performance or the mark given for the assessment. You may also decide to arrange a social event to celebrate the end of the presentation which can be an opportunity for apologizing or forgiving any arguments or bad behaviour in the group. It is usually best to bring some closure on anything that has been negative. Celebrate finishing the presentation and move on.

Consider the composition of the group

In student situations, you may have no control over the composition of your group. In some situations you may be asked to form groups of a set number. This approach is often used when you have been on a course for several months or years and have worked together previously. An alternative approach is where you are given the list of the people you will be working with. The tutor may have chosen this method to save the time wasted while everyone decides who wants to work with whom! This approach is often used at conferences or at the start of academic courses when students do not know anyone else on the course. In these examples, names may have been randomly allocated to the different groups.

It is useful to think about the group members from two perspectives:

1 Strangers or friends.
2 Similar or different individuals.

Strangers or friends   If the group is a collection of strangers you will need to use different techniques to work well together than if you are with friends or colleagues who you have worked with before. With strangers you will not know their strengths and what they can bring to the group and some time may be needed to exchange names and background experience. Different amounts of time will be needed for the first three stages of group development outlined above. If you are strangers, the forming and storming stages will need some time before you reach the norming stage. However, if you are friends or have already worked together, you will probably reach stage three quite quickly.

Similar or different individuals   Another feature of group membership is if you are all similar (a homogeneous group) or quite different (a heterogeneous group). For student presentations, it is probable that you will share several features such as being on the same course or the same module, however beyond that there may be very few similarities. Some academic courses have full- and part-time students and this combination can be a feature in group work. Understandably, part-time students will have limited time for planning meetings so e-mail communication will probably become the main channel for communicating. This diversity through age, ethnicity, gender and experience can provide opportunities for developing your people skills. We have seen groups where young students work alongside older members who indeed may be a similar age to their parents. For successful group work, each person will need to respect the others' position. The most experienced member may need to learn to hold back from making all of the suggestions and encourage the younger members to contribute. In contrast, the younger members will need to be willing to learn from the more experienced members yet be assertive enough to make their ideas heard and understood.

The diversity of the group can certainly contribute to its effectiveness and success and a range of skills and personalities will enrich the presentation. Adair (1986) identified several characteristics that individuals can contribute to effective teams. These included:

- The ability to work as a team member
- Suitable levels of professional and technical competence
- A willingness to listen and learn from other people
- A flexible outlook
- The ability to give and accept trust

All these are a combination of personality traits, skills and experience. Although you may hope that the other members of the group will have these characteristics, it is useful to think about your own contribution to effective group working. Which characteristics do you need to improve so that you are a better team player? It is also important to accept that being friends with the other members will not automatically make group working more effective. In fact this can sometimes add to problems in the group. Learning to work well in a team is useful experience for your employment situations.

Assign roles and responsibilities within the group

For most student presentations, there is not much time to work on the presentation so assigning a different role to each group member can save time and make everyone take some responsibility for contributing to the final event. In our research the students thought assigning different roles was important because it helped them to have a clear framework for working together. It helped them to understand what they were supposed to be doing and make each individual contribution visible. These students reported that after working on a few presentations, they knew what they were best at and what skills they could contribute to the presentation. However, they also believed that as they became more confident, they were willing to take on new roles or share these with other students so that their skills continued to develop.

For some presentations it may be best to use a thematic approach where you divide the topic to be covered into suitable themes. Each member creates the content for their allocated theme. In this way, you all use a range of roles to complete your content and spend time during meetings and rehearsals to put the individual contributions together to produce a cohesive presentation.

An alternative approach is where the roles are assigned and then content is developed within the constraints of these roles. Research by Belbin (1981) into effective management teams identified as many as eight roles that could be used in a team. Many of his suggested roles are not relevant to group presentations but the principle of developing roles and allocating them to different members is a useful approach for group work. It makes individual contributions more visible in the group and helps progress to be made. For a student presentation, fewer roles will probably be needed and the size of the group will influence the number but it might be useful to consider the following roles as useful for your situation:

Leader or co-ordinator   The need for a group leader will depend on the circumstances. You may not want to give a bossy person the opportunity to dominate the work of the group but a leader can be useful to provide direction and co-ordination of the work you are doing. Some of our students believed that nominating a leader during the first meeting was important and helped to get the work going more quickly for the presentation. They also thought it created a clear line of communication for group members. Having a leader can sometimes prevent different factions forming in the group as the leader becomes the focal point for communication and co-ordination.

Choosing a leader can sometimes create problems. How the leader is chosen may be influenced by how well you know each other. If you have worked together before, you may choose someone with proven leadership abilities who can motivate everyone. If you work together frequently, you can rotate the leader's role giving each member an opportunity to develop their leadership skills.

Another approach to consider if you have already worked together on several tasks is to choose a spokesperson to represent the group but take a strong team approach. Each member accepts clear responsibility for specific tasks and a communication network is set up where everyone reports their progress and advises or supports each other. This is an egalitarian approach that works well when there is a strong degree of trust within the group.

If you are working with strangers, it is more difficult to appoint a leader. It can be useful to suggest that members volunteer for the role. Ask each volunteer to describe briefly their plans for what needs to be prepared for the presentation. In a large group everyone could then vote for a preferred choice. In a small group this could be achieved through consensus. As the discussion evolves some volunteers may withdraw or suggest one of the other volunteers is more suitable and a compromise can be agreed. This will avoid a contest for the group leader. Whichever method you use, try to make sure that the process of choosing a leader does not become more important than starting work for the presentation.

When the leader is chosen use the role of leader wisely. They should not be blamed for whatever goes wrong, nor should they claim the credit for all of the successes. Leading a student group requires vision, determination and sensitivity. You may be the leader for working on the group presentation but you will revert to being an ordinary member of the cohort for the rest of your course. If you fall out with other students it can be unpleasant for everyone in the group or in other modules on the course. Good communication is the key to success here. The leader needs to make sure each member has a clear understanding of their role and the tasks involved. Agree time scales and dates for completing these tasks. Emphasize the value of teamwork rather than encouraging a hierarchy to develop in the group. The final presentation will be much better if you have worked well as a team.

Researcher   In many group situations, all members should be doing some research for the content of the presentation. However, having one person responsible for locating the relevant sources of information can help to prevent duplication of effort. The Researcher can co-ordinate the individual research results and gathers copies of items needed through libraries, organizations or websites. This person needs to record the searches they have made and useful information that has been found. They also need the ability to think laterally when considering the range of possible information sources available. Finally, they need tenacity. They must not give up easily but keep searching and following any possible ideas and leads that may prove useful. Tutors see many student presentations that appear similar. Finding interesting and unusual content and examples can make a more memorable presentation that earns higher marks for originality.

Resource investigator and gatherer   This role can be combined with the role of Researcher. However the main purpose is to find the different resources needed to complete the presentation. These can be for developing the content such as IT labs or software packages. Resources could also be needed for the presentation event such as demonstration models, free copies of examples available from organizations or copies of handouts for the audience. This person is also responsible for any negotiations needed to use these resources and to make sure they are stored safely and available for the actual presentation event. In media organizations, this role is sometimes referred to as a 'Gofer'. It needs a lateral thinker, someone who enjoys the challenges of communicating outside of the group and negotiating with a wider range of individuals. As for the Researcher, the Resource Investigator also needs tenacity to make sure they find and deliver what is needed.

Note taker or administrator   This role can be especially important in the planning stages of the group working together. In a small group, it can be combined with other roles. It is essential to record any decisions made and the areas of responsibility or the roles agreed. In some situations this person could take minutes of the meetings but most student group situations will probably not need this formal recording. The student who accepts this role will need to be methodical, pay attention to detail and be efficient in how they prepare minutes, store records and communicate with other group members. It may be possible in a small group to merge this role with the one below.

Writer or content developer   Again, this can be shared between members and if this is the case then this role would become more of an editor of the combined content. If they have sole responsibility for content development then all ideas and information resources will need to be shared and discussed and the content agreed on by all or most of the group members. It is wise to build in time for a review of content where feedback can be incorporated so that every member feels some ownership for it. This person needs good communication and listening skills. They should have good writing techniques and the ability to create content under pressure to meet deadlines. However, they will need to be careful not to claim ownership of the presentation just because they developed the content. They will need to retain a strong team focus and recognize the contributions from the other members.

PowerPoint developer   Like all of the other roles some tasks for this can be shared, but having one person with overall responsibility will help to achieve some consistency of content and style. Many students will have had some experience of creating a PowerPoint presentation and we discuss this in much more detail in Chapter 9. For this role the person needs the right level of technical skills but they also need to be good at creating a clear presentation from a larger volume of content, another example of good communication skills. Additional supporting materials such as more detailed handouts can be created by other members for the audience but a succinct and attractive PowerPoint presentation will considerably improve the final event.

Create a listening and decision-making culture

This can be difficult to create, especially in student groups where you will probably have equal status on your course. The group leader can take some responsibility for creating this culture. Ground rules will need to be laid down at the start of the group working together and all members will need to accept them. These could include basic behaviours such as:

- not interrupting when a member is outlining an idea
- making sure that everyone makes a contribution to the discussion
- taking turns to make these contributions
- encouraging members to think about ideas before group meetings so that they bring better suggestions to the group discussions
- only allowing negative comments if they are given with a constructive comment or solution to a problem

- allowing a discussion period for ideas then moving towards a consensus so that work can progress
- asking if anyone has anything else to say before each meeting finishes

Set clear group and individual goals

Having a clear set of group goals provides a useful framework for group working. These goals need to cover all aspects of performance which contribute to the overall effectiveness of the group. This sounds like management jargon and may seem confusing but it can be quite straightforward. Goals are tasks that need to be completed. The briefing for the presentation should describe what you have to do for your presentation. Using these as the end goals for the group, you then think about the essential tasks needed to get to these end goals. You may find it useful to follow these next stages:

1. As a group you could make a list of everything that needs to be done for the presentation.
2. Group the tasks into similar themes or activities. An example could be creating the PowerPoint slides linked to creating the handouts for the audience. Another example could be booking a room then making sure that the technology was available such as an overhead projector or access to a computer.
3. Assign the tasks to different group members and agree dates for completion.
4. Check the balance of the workload and dates to make sure that no member has too much to do in a short amount of time.
5. Ask members to report on their progress for each of their tasks at group meetings or through the agreed communication channels of e-mails or texts.
6. Use group meetings to discuss any problems that have arisen for these tasks, review progress and give feedback on the quality of work and any features that need to be improved.

If you have assigned roles to each group member then the different tasks that need to be completed tend to fall naturally into these roles.

Make individual performance visible to the group

Much of the conflict in groups is due to the varying contributions from members so that some students think they are working harder and contributing more to the presentation than other group members. To reduce this conflict, it is important to plan how different member contributions can be identified and co-ordinated towards achieving the group goal.

If you follow the stages outlined above, the contributions will become visible as each person reports on their progress. However, being visible does mean that those who have not made much progress should be asked to explain why. If problems are identified then another member may be able to share some of the responsibility for a task and a review of workloads can help to prevent some members doing too much.

If a member fails to turn up to meetings or frequently uses excuses for not completing any tasks, then the group will need to think about how to deal with this to minimize the damage. Do you expel them from the group? Do you tell the tutor or compensate by working even harder yourself? Only you can decide. It can be upsetting when you have worked hard on your tasks but others have not and you begin to worry that the final quality of the presentation will be reduced. It may not be possible to compensate for the reduced performance of some members. Nevertheless, making individual goals visible to the whole group can help to show the value of each member's contribution to the final event. This may help the tutor to evaluate the individual performances, even when there is a group mark. Sharing the group mark is more likely to cause problems when it represents a high proportion of the total marks for a module. When the group presentation mark is 30 per cent or less of the total mark, you may work harder to raise your final module total by improving your score for the individual piece of work. However, there are situations when the group work earns the total mark and you just have to make sure the group performance earns at least the same as you would probably earn if working alone.

Deal constructively with conflict or failure

Conflict in groups can be very upsetting and leave you feeling angry or disillusioned. Most of us find dealing with conflict difficult. Several of our students said that trying to sort out problems in the group was a distraction from the real purpose of the group working together. Sometimes they did not feel confident enough to challenge the trouble makers or those members who made only a small contribution compared with some other members. There are several ways to deal with group problems.

If the group has a leader, they will need to find out the true reasons for the problems and the perceptions of different members. They could then choose one of two broad approaches to dealing with conflict, a dictatorial approach or a consultative approach. For the dictatorial approach, the leader consults with the members individually then decides on the course of action and explains it to the rest of the group who have to accept the decision or leave the group. This could work where the leader has clear authority and respect from the group members. However, in many student group situations, this could risk alienating most of the group.

For the consultative approach, the leader gathers everyone in the group together to discuss the problems and the reasons for them with the aim of resolving the differences.

Some ground rules need to be set at the start of the meeting where the emphasis is on solving problems rather than blaming different individuals. Each member should have the opportunity to outline the problems from their perspective and nobody else can interrupt them. This is followed by a discussion that concentrates on possible solutions. This approach will need strong direction and co-ordination from the leader but may result in better outcomes than the first approach.

Tutors may be unaware of problems in the groups or may refuse to intervene. It may be worth asking for their help but only you will be able to decide if this will be worthwhile. Sometimes, it can seem to be admitting failure by asking for their help. Group conflict can be unpleasant and should be avoided if possible but it can also be a learning experience. If reflection and review of the final presentation are included in the work schedule, there can be opportunities to discuss what worked well and aspects of the group work that could be improved for a future occasion. Whilst the group may never work together again, this reflection can help to prevent the members making the same mistakes in the future. We all have negative experiences in group working; it is a natural consequence of humans working together. However the experience can be useful if we learn from it and take away something positive that can be used in future group situations. We discuss learning through the presentation in Chapter 10. We conclude this chapter by summarizing key principles that contribute to effective group work for presentations.

KEY PRINCIPLES FOR EFFECTIVE GROUP WORK

1   Create roles with responsibilities for each group member.
2   Develop group and individual goals that are achievable.
3   Design tasks that contribute to these goals.
4   Set up communication systems between members to report on progress or problems.
5   Create a listening culture in the group where ideas can be considered openly and developed rather than immediately dismissed.
6   Deal with conflict constructively. Develop acceptable behaviours in group meetings that encourage lively discussion but prevent a culture of blame or loss of face for some individuals.
7   Make decisions after considering all options and through consensus in the group so that each member supports these decisions.
8   Make individual performance visible to the rest of the group.
9   Create methods of feedback for individual and group performance that encourage raising standards.
10 Aim to enjoy the experience and learn something from the experience, even if there are problems.

References

Adair, J. (1986) *Effective Team Building.* Aldershot: Gower.

Belbin, M. (1981) *Management Teams.* Oxford: Butterworth.

Cyert, R. M. and March, J. E. (1963) *A Behavioural Theory of The Firm.* Englewood Cliffs, NJ: Prentice Hall.

Diehl, M. and Stroebe, W. (1987) 'Productivity loss in brainstorming groups: toward the solution of a riddle', *Journal of Personality and Social Psychology,* 53: 497–509.

Janis, I. L. (1982) *Groupthink: A Study of Foreign Policy Decisions and Fiascos,* 2nd edn. Boston: Houghton Mifflin.

Janis, I. L. (1989) *Crucial Decisions.* New York: Free Press.

Myers, D. G. and Lamm, H. (1976) 'The group polarization phenomenon', *Psychological Bulletin,* 83: 602–27.

Rogelberg, S. G., Barnes-Farrell, J.L. and Lowe, C.A. (1992) 'The stepladder technique: an alternative group structure facilitating effective group decision-making', *Journal of Applied Psychology,* 77: 730–7.

Tuckman, B. and Jensen, M. (1977) 'Stages of small group development', *Groups and Organizational Studies,* 2: 419–27.

5 Ten Steps for Preparing your Presentation

LEARNING OBJECTIVES

Reading this chapter will help you to:

- understand the importance of planning for your presentation
- use your time effectively to reduce the stress
- research the content of the presentation
- follow the ten-step plan for your presentation

Good preparation and planning are essential for successful presentations. The quality of your presentation usually reflects the amount of preparation you have done. Many students feel overwhelmed with the work needed for a presentation and may not know how to approach the task. Some students underestimate the amount of preparation needed and leave this work until a few days before the scheduled date. Both of these approaches can cause stress but some of this stress can be reduced if you follow the ten-step plan that we suggest below.

1 Read and re-read the briefing details for the presentation.
2 Create a task list or mind map.
3 Create a time chart.
4 Review your existing knowledge of the topic.
5 Research and read to gain new knowledge.
6 Decide on the balance of the content.
7 Find relevant examples.
8 Identify your audience.
9 Create the content, visual aids and documentation.
10 Rehearse the presentation.

Some of these tasks will only take a short amount of time while others will take longer or be ongoing throughout the preparation period. From this list you will see that creating and writing the content are listed as number nine and you might think this is too late in the sequence of tasks. You should not interpret this as waiting to create the content until just before the presentation event. All of the previous tasks feed into the content creation.

We think reviewing your progress should be an ongoing task. As you work through the stages outlined above, you will gain a clearer sense of the tasks needed and should be able to identify more realistic time frames. Ongoing reviews will make you aware of your progress or lack of progress and should help you to improve your motivation and time management.

Some of these tasks are covered in much more detail in later chapters and we give links to these when relevant. However, you might find it useful to review these tasks before you choose to read any of these other chapters.

1   Read and re-read the briefing details for the presentation

This may seem obvious but we have had many experiences where the presentations have been interesting but the students have not actually done what was asked of them. Because of this, we suggest that your first step should be to read the briefing sheet to make sure that you fully understand what you have to do. Look at how the marks are allocated if it is an assessed presentation. Think about what you can do and how you can do it well so that you can earn a good mark. Most tutors will be happy to answer your questions so if you are unsure of any of the details ask them to explain it more clearly. Usually, if you are not sure about something, there will also be other students feeling the same.

If the presentation is for a job interview, as in Example 6 in Chapter 1, try to make sure that you have a clear understanding of what the panel expect from you. If the details are open or rather vague, decide how you are going to fulfil the task and include a brief description of your approach in the introduction.

2   Create a task list or mind map

Creating this list or a mind map will be easier as you gain more experience of presentations but in most situations, it will be useful to think about all of the tasks that need to be completed for the presentation. You will probably only need to spend a few minutes on this stage of your preparation. The list of tasks will vary according to the type and purpose of the presentation but if you find it difficult to create your own list, you could use these general headings as a working framework.

- Research the topic
- Read and develop the content

- Create visual aids and documentation
- Review and rehearse the presentation

We list these headings in their expected order of progress. However most of these tasks will be ongoing and may need to be reviewed regularly. If you prefer working with mind maps then this is a useful stage to create one as a working document.

An alternative list of working headings could be those we have used for this chapter. You can use these whether you are working alone or in a group:

- Create a task list
- Create a time chart
- Review your existing knowledge
- Research and read to gain new knowledge
- Decide on the balance of the content
- Find relevant examples
- Identify your audience
- Prepare the content, visual aids and documentation
- Rehearse the presentation

These take a similar approach by listing the tasks in a natural sequence of progression but they are more specific in how they define the work needed to be completed. If you are the type of person who works well with lists, you may find these useful. However, if long lists create stress for you, the first set may be a more useful framework to use.

Whichever approach you take, having an order of priority will help to create a structure to your preparation and a realization of what can be achieved in the time available. Your chosen list can also be used to keep you motivated as it may be satisfying to see completed tasks and recognize that you are making progress with the work involved.

As you continue with your preparation, more detailed tasks within each general heading will be identified. An example of this could be under the heading in the second list for 'Finding relevant examples', and you might list:

1 Search the web for relevant organizations.
2 Contact the organization for brochures.
3 Create Case Study profiles.
4 Decide how to use these examples in the presentation.

It can be easy to become distracted by the lists or mind maps and give them more time than the actual preparation work for the presentation so do use them carefully.

However, these lists and maps will probably be useful when you are working on several assignments at one time. You could also use them if you are asked to give a progress report to your tutor or for group work when you hold progress review meetings and re-allocate tasks to different members.

See Chapter 7 for more discussion on developing content by using mind maps.

3   Create a time chart

Good time management is a very important part of the preparation period. It is useful to remember that you will need time for researching the topic, learning and understanding new knowledge as well as for creating the content of the presentation. We suggest that you take some time to consider the following points:

1   Look at the overall time between receiving the briefing for the presentation and the actual date of delivery. This may vary between perhaps two weeks to several months.
2   Create an overall time list where you use the generic headings we suggest above: research the topic, reading and developing content, creating visual aids and documentation, review and rehearsal. This could be developed by week rather than by actual date.
3   Now think about your commitments to lectures and other work during this time period. The actual free time to work on the preparation, in a three-month period, may be limited to just a few days or even a few hours.
4   Identify where these free time slots are and how many hours they will be. This will help to remind you that preparation work should begin immediately. Also, if you are aware of when these occur in your schedule, you will be more likely to use them to work on your presentation. The amount of free time in each slot can also influence the tasks you choose at this time. One hour may give you the chance to use a library or search the web to find useful sources of information but a few hours can be used to read, think and write the content.
5   Next create a second time list using these dates and tasks to be achieved. It may be useful to build in some slippage time for unexpected problems or delays. You can create these lists by using Microsoft Word or Excel and edit them as you make progress. If you use a diary a general list can be made in the diary with tasks allocated to specific dates and times. If you use a mind map, dates can be included as the map develops.

These five tasks may only take you 30 minutes but it will be time well spent. As the preparation progresses you will need to review your progress. This is especially crucial for group presentations and we discuss this in more detail in Chapter 4. However, it is also essential when you are working alone and will help you to incorporate delays from unexpected events, adapt the content or make the necessary changes. We hope it will also help to reduce your panic and work more effectively towards the final delivery of your presentation.

4   Review your existing knowledge of the topic

This may seem an obvious or unnecessary stage of the preparation and will be influenced directly by your circumstances. We discuss this briefly here but Chapter 7 will be useful to help you with this stage of your presentation.

The type and purpose of your presentation will influence this stage of your preparation. If you are presenting your own research, you will almost certainly know and understand the topic so will need to move to step five for deciding the balance of the content you will present. If you have been given the topic by a lecturer, or chosen it from a list provided by the lecturer you will need to take a different approach. For this scenario you may have very little knowledge or interest in the topic but you will need to develop this during the preparation period. The following processes will help you.

- Collect together your existing notes on the topic. Scan the material that you have collected already. If you have photocopies, printouts or lecture notes, divide them into piles to develop a working framework. You may find it useful to use adhesive labels to add comments about why an article could be useful.
- Reflect on what you know already. You may have a general overview that has been developed from earlier modules or lectures. This overview may be enough to hold a conversation with a colleague or friend but insufficient for a formal presentation to a mixed audience or group of experts. You will need to sound informed and knowledgeable rather than naïve and superficial. The content will need to have some strength and depth to earn a reasonable mark.
- Write down what you already know about the subject. You probably know more than you think. Use either a notepad or your computer, whichever you prefer, to write down ideas and connections. If you have a strongly visual imagination, use drawings, mind maps, pictures or doodles to help generate ideas and make connections.

5   Research and read to gain new knowledge

There are many different ways to research a topic and you will probably have already developed your preferred approach while working on assignments. We discuss this in more detail in Chapter 7.

Gaining new knowledge is an important and essential preparation stage and usually takes more time than you think it will. We have found that when students feel a sense of panic at this stage, it helps them to first re-read their lecture notes and handouts. We then encourage them to read any recommended readings given for the module or the topic that will be relevant. Finally, we suggest they read the new resources they have found from their research. This does seem to be a rather tedious approach but it can help you if you feel overwhelmed by your lack of knowledge. If you think you do already have a reasonable understanding of the topic, perhaps you can re-read a few relevant handouts and then move on quickly to read the new items found in your research.

In other words, to gain new knowledge on a topic, you need to read yourself into it. To understand new knowledge, it usually takes more than one read and to understand it well enough to present on the topic it will probably take two or three readings. This is why we stressed earlier how important it is to allocate your time well. Reading can seem to be a slow process and for many people the preparation tasks linked to presentations are thought to be the 'doing' tasks, such as creating handouts and a PowerPoint presentation, rather than the more intellectual tasks of reading, thinking and learning.

All of this research and reading will help you to decide what the presentation should be about and what you need to know before you can deliver it. As the content begins to take shape in your mind, you can add more detail to your lists or mind maps and begin to create and organize the content. We look at this in the next section.

6   Decide on the balance of the content

This will be influenced by the academic context and purpose of the presentation and the intended audience. You may need to decide between a big picture approach and one that selects a smaller area with more detail. As you develop your knowledge of the topic, you will feel more confident about what to include and what to leave out. You will also be able to decide what is best covered through speech, text, images and what could be given in a handout rather than used as presentation content.

In many academic situations, we would expect your academic tutor to provide some guidance on this balance and emphasis of the expected content. This might be given in a tutorial or in the briefing instructions so do check if this support is available to you.

As your knowledge develops, you will begin to identify the main themes and issues around the topic. These could be:

- different perspectives or the current situation in contrast to earlier approaches
- what recent research evidence is available

- how government or international policies are impacting on the topic
- new trends that are emerging
- forecasts for the future

7 Find relevant examples

It will be useful during your preparation and research to find several examples you can use to improve the audience understanding of your content. These may be organizations, individuals or incidents reported in the literature or experiences that you or members of the audience may have had. You could choose examples of poor or good practice but you will need to think about how these are used and how much anonymity will be needed. Sometimes, finding examples can improve your own interest and help you to understand the topic at a deeper level.

In the section on creating a task list or mind map, we showed how this task of finding relevant examples could be further divided so we repeat them here to remind you how to collect these examples:

1 Search the web for relevant organizations.
2 Contact the organization for brochures.
3 Create Case Study profiles.
4 Decide how you will use these examples in the presentation.

We emphasize this as a task in the preparation stage because it is easier to gather these examples as an ongoing task rather than trying to find them towards the end of your preparation period. Sometimes, it takes quite a long time from contacting an organization for information to actually receiving it. Fortunately, more information is now available on the web, but in our experience many good examples have not been included in student presentations due to the late arrival of suitable information. By allowing plenty of time, you will be able to feel in control of your chosen examples. As your research progresses, earlier examples can be replaced by better ones but being aware of these will almost certainly improve your own understanding of the topic area and the relevance to the context of the module.

8 Identify your audience

We discuss the audience in more detail in Chapter 6. However, during the preparation stages it is useful to remind yourself regularly of who will be listening to and watching the presentation. Again, this will be influenced by the academic context and for some situations this stage of your preparation will require no real effort on your part or be beyond your control.

Getting to know something about your audience before the event may actually make you feel more nervous. Because of this, you need to make sure that this part of the preparation is useful and helps you to shape the content with the audience in mind. As your work progresses, knowledge of the expected audience and the resulting focus of the content will probably help to reduce your nerves.

If you are giving a presentation at a conference or for a job interview, it will be useful to spend some time finding out whether the audience will be novices or experts. If they are novices, think about how you will develop their knowledge of the topic in a short space of time.

What will they need to know or find useful to know?
How can you make the content interesting to them?
How much useful interaction can you expect from them?
Will they be active, for example by doing exercises, or more passive through sitting, watching and listening?

If they are experts, consider the following questions:

What will be their experience of the topic?
What levels of knowledge will they already have?
Why will they be at the presentation – to assess you in some way or to gain new knowedge?

Many student presentations are delivered in front of other students on the module and this may make you nervous. Some students may prefer presenting to strangers rather than to colleagues. However, in these circumstances it can be useful to remember that if they are also delivering a presentation, they will probably be nervous, less judgmental and more empathic than strangers.

Identifying the audience will also help you to decide what type and style of performance you will need to give and we discussed this in Chapter 3. You may also need to think about what your audience needs to learn from the presentation. If you are presenting content that is part of a module curriculum they will probably feel grateful if your presentation has some meaning for them and is easy to understand. This is discussed in Chapter 10. Who the audience are will also influence the type of supporting documentation that you will need to create and this is covered in Chapter 8.

9 Create the content, visual aids and documentation

This is a very important stage of your preparation, even though this is the penultimate task on our list. All of the previous tasks feed into this stage which will be easier if you have carried out some good research and reading on the topic.

You will probably need to allow quite a lot of time during the preparation period to create the content and the supporting documents required for your presentation. The type and purpose will inevitably influence what you create at this stage. You may need to create three types of documents here:

- The script
- A PowerPoint presentation
- Handouts for the audience

The script

For Example 2 in Chapter 1, a seminar presentation, you may be asked to write a paper that you read aloud and submit for assessment. For this example, some very detailed content will be needed and the preparation will probably seem similar to other types of assignment such as an essay or report.

Some students find it useful to write a script for any type of presentation, even if they will not read the script word for word. They use it as a prompt or as something to rely on if they get really nervous and forget everything they intended to say. You may choose to do this or you may prefer to only write an overview of the structure and use bullet points for the key themes that you intend to cover. You should create whatever you need to perform to the best of your capability.

A PowerPoint presentation

You will also need to decide on the type of visual aids and documents needed and allocate a realistic amount of time to fulfil this task. If you are working in a group the task of creating the PowerPoint presentation can be delegated to one or two of the members after most of the content has been developed. We discuss this in more detail in Chapter 9.

Handouts for the audience

If you intend to provide copies of the PowerPoint slides, creating handouts from these is a simple stage of the process. However, if you are asked to give more detailed handouts, then you will need extra time to create these from the range of resources used in your research. You may be able to include these as notes pages within the PowerPoint or you may decide to create them as separate text files.

If you are expected to provide a list of references or a bibliography of further readings, this will also take some time to prepare, but these documents can evolve as your research and content develop. Start a file for this and add items as the research progresses.

Remember to include some time for editing the content and documents and for creating the correct number of copies needed. Most people end up with more content than they can use in the time available. Chapters 7, 8 and 9 discuss creating and structuring content and explore how to develop visual aids and supporting documentation.

10   Rehearse the presentation

We believe it is essential to include rehearsal in the stages of preparation. In our experience, students have tended to spend time on the planning and some research but frequently deliver the presentation without much rehearsal. Even if the content is good, the overall impression of the presentation may only be average if there is insufficient rehearsal. The benefits of rehearsal cannot be overemphasized and the following advice may be useful for increasing your confidence and reducing some of the stress. Rather than seeing rehearsal as something to try to fit in if you have the time, break it into smaller areas for rehearsal under the following themes which are also discussed in Chapter 3.

Rehearsal checklist

- Rehearse and learn the factual content and structure so that they are very familiar to you. Make sure that you understand the wider context of the topic so that you will be able to handle questions effectively.
- Rehearse speaking aloud so that you can hear the sound level, pitch and emphasis you need to use in your voice. This will help you to use pauses confidently and prevent you from rushing in to fill the silences that do occur naturally in presentations.
- Rehearse in front of a mirror or video camera so that you can see how members of the audience will see you. This may cause you to change the way that you use your hands or how you hold your notes or cards. Using a mirror or video is a technique used by many actors and professional communicators and can improve your performance considerably.
- Time the rehearsals so that you can edit your content to fit the time available. You may be penalized for taking longer than the time given or you may be told to stop when the

allotted time is up, regardless of how little of the content you have covered. Rehearsal should help you to be realistic about what you can reasonably be expected to cover and what content could be given in a handout.

- Rehearse as part of the group to make sure that it sounds like one complete presentation rather than a set of individual parts with some duplication. Group rehearsal will also help to prevent the presentation overrunning for the reasons we have outlined above.
- Rehearse using the technology to improve your skills and confidence levels. This will also help you to be time efficient. Using the technology should not delay your progress but improve the overall quality. This rehearsal will also help you to be aware of how much movement is needed to operate the technology.
- Rehearse in the physical environment if this is possible. Practice in using tables, lecterns or chairs will be a real help for the actual event. Think about whether you will be sitting or standing during the presentation and which will be the most appropriate for the event. Will you need to move around the room or be expected to remain in one place?

A well rehearsed presentation will improve both your performance and enjoyment of the event. It will help to reduce your nerves and increase your confidence on the day.

Rehearsal may also help to improve your understanding of the content and enable you to answer questions more competently. Improved confidence may help you to be more analytical and objective about your performance. You should be able to understand what worked well, and what could be improved. Individual or group reflection of the event will help to ensure that you learn from the presentation experience and improve your performance in future presentations.

KEY PRINCIPLES FOR PREPARING YOUR PRESENTATION

1 See effective planning as an essential part of preparing for the presentation.
2 Be realistic about the amount of free time that you have to prepare the presentation so that you use this time effectively.
3 Use some of the preparation period to carry out your research and read to improve your knowledge and understanding of the topic.
4 Think about the purpose of the presentation and who your audience will be. This will help to make sure the presentation has the correct emphasis and achieves the aims set by the tutor.
5 Create interesting content with good examples and a clear structure that fits the time you have been given for the presentation and stimulates discussion.
6 Rehearse your presentation several times so that you will be more confident when you deliver it.

Further reading

Bell, Judith (2005) *Doing your Research Project: a Guide for First-time Researchers in Education, Health and Social Science*, 4th edn. Maidenhead: Open University Press.

Buzan, Tony (2003) *The Mind Map Book*. London: BBC Active.

Denscombe, Martyn (2003) *The Good Research Guide*, 2nd edn. Maidenhead: Open University Press.

6 Understanding your Audience

LEARNING OBJECTIVES

Reading this chapter will help you to:

- consider a range of audience perspectives on a presentation
- understand how the audience influences your presentation
- develop a presentation that meets the needs of the audience

For many student presentations, the audience is an important factor and we think it will be useful for you to give it some special consideration in this chapter. We use the term 'audience' to include anyone who is watching your presentation. This could be friends, colleagues or strangers who have several different roles, such as tutors, examiners, conference delegates or members of an interview panel.

Throughout this book, we have encouraged you to consider your audience at all of the stages of preparing and delivering your presentation. We have already discussed how audiences can influence presentations in several chapters. In each of the examples we use in Chapter 1 the likely audience has been included. In Chapter 2 we discuss involving the audience in the presentation to make it more effective. Chapter 3 encourages you to rehearse and consider how the audience will understand the content through the quality of your presentation. In Chapter 5 we discuss identifying your audience as one of the preparation stages because they will probably have some influence on the content and style of the presentation. This would certainly be the case for an interview as outlined in example 6 in Chapter 1. We also encourage you to think about the audience when you prepare the supporting documentation discussed in Chapter 8. Thinking about how the audience learns from your presentation is considered in Chapter 10. We make all these links to remind you how important the audience can be when preparing and delivering your presentation.

This chapter provides a focus on the different facets of your audience. To present successfully, you need to think about how the audience will see you and about their roles and motives for watching your presentation.

Features to consider about the audience

There are numerous features that you need to think about and we discuss these under the following headings:

- Size of the audience
- Composition of the audience
- Reasons and purpose for being there

Size of the audience

It helps in the planning stages if you find out the expected number of people who will attend the presentation. Practical preparation tasks such as setting out the room or preparing the correct number of handouts are made easier. A large audience can make you more nervous than a small one but preparing for a large audience will be less of a shock than if it was unexpected. Some university courses ask all final year students to deliver a presentation on their dissertation to tutors and all final year students. In this situation, you will be able to anticipate the audience size and the presentation will probably be quite formal. It is useful to expect that a larger audience will need a more formal style of presentation. The exception is for an interview where there could only be three or four people watching but it is a formal occasion.

Composition of the audience

Think about what the people in the audience have in common. This can be many aspects such as all being students of the same module on a course or a professional group such as health workers, teachers, psychologists, social workers or physicists. This will help you to be aware of their level of skills, knowledge and experience such as whether they are experts or novices. It can also be useful to think of their age, cultural and social factors. All these factors will influence the content and style of your presentation and how you communicate with your audience. This will also help you to plan for how much participation you can expect. Whilst you can develop exercises for other students or people with a similar knowledge, it can be less advisable to use these exercises with experts. An exception could be when you are making an important point that perhaps they need to become aware of through the exercise. There is also much evidence to show that with novices you provide strong conclusions to your topic, but for experts you leave the conclusions more open for them to reflect on and develop themselves.

Reasons and purpose for being there

Think about why the audience is watching your presentation. All of the examples in Chapter 1 explain the role of the audience in the presentation. Consider if their attendance is compulsory or voluntary. Do they need to learn, to buy something, to be inspired and motivated, or do they perhaps have to assess your performance such as in a Viva as in Example 1 or decide if they should offer you a job as in Example 6? In both of these examples, there is much to gain and lose, so the quality of your presentation is very important. You will probably have a very short amount of time to give a convincing performance of your knowledge and ability. The reason why the audience is watching your presentation will influence their mindset and attitude towards you, their level of interest in the topic and in your presentation skills.

Understanding their reasons for being there will help you to understand what they need from the presentation. This understanding will help you to meet their needs and make their attendance worthwhile. Include the audience in your planning stages. Most people are very busy but are likely to enjoy an interesting presentation where they learn something new or useful.

Audience perspectives on your presentation

One of the values of considering your audience in this chapter is that it reminds you there will be different views on the effectiveness and value of your presentation. Student presentations can usually be viewed from several perspectives and we discuss three of these below:

- Student audience
- Tutor audience
- Employer

Student audience

The student audience may be influenced by how much they enjoy seeing their peers performing in a stressful situation, or how much empathy they feel, knowing that it will be their turn soon. If students are watching several presentations, they may become bored but they will certainly make comparisons between their own presentations and yours.

The student audience will also be influenced by their level of understanding, interest and enjoyment of the subject and by how useful it has been for their learning. In some situations, the tutor may encourage these students to concentrate on the content rather than the performance and in these circumstances students may be less judgmental of the level of presentation skills and more critical of the content. However, the reverse can also happen in academic situations for drama and the performing arts where the performance is central to the event.

It will probably be useful for you to think about some of the student presentations that you have watched and what was interesting about them. How much did you learn about the topic? What improvements would you suggest to improve the presentation? Putting yourself in the audience's chair can be a very useful exercise for improving your own performance.

Tutor audience

For many student presentations, tutors will be a part of the audience and when these presentations are assessed, the tutor's perspective will probably be the most important. The marks for your presentation can contribute to your total mark for the modules as in Examples 2 and 3 in Chapter 1. On some final year modules, this mark will contribute to the final degree classification as in Example 1. Increasingly, students are given detailed briefings on what is expected of these assessed presentations and what proportion of the marks will be awarded. Marks will vary between different courses but tutors will probably be looking for a range of features including:

- how the presentation fulfils the purpose of the exercise
- the type and level of content and how this is structured
- the presentation and communication skills of the presenter
- the amount of originality in the chosen approach
- how well the presenters appear to understand the topic
- the quality and detail of answers to the questions at the end of the presentation. This is an essential part of the presentation when it is a Viva or an interview.

Experienced tutors will use presentations as opportunities for your learning and development far beyond the formal assessment criteria. Some students think doing presentations is a method for moving the pressures of teaching from the tutor to the student. However, this is rarely true because tutors find managing student presentations very time consuming and challenging, especially in a large cohort with several groups working together. Student presentations still need support and guidance from tutors. Presentations need very clear briefing for the students, who usually need some extra advice during the preparation time.

Presentations are now a regular feature on many student courses. We discussed the benefits to students in Chapter 1 but students are often worried about what a tutor will be looking for and how they will be marked. Even when formal assessment criteria are given to students, they often ask tutors what will earn high marks or what the benefits are for their tutors. Reflecting briefly on some benefits for tutors may help you to understand why presentations are used so frequently in learning situations. This will help you to make better use of the opportunities that presentations offer. Benefits for tutors can be summarized as:

- awareness of student group dynamics
- deeper knowledge of individual students
- new knowledge and finding out what students know
- exchanging roles with the student
- experiencing the physical learning environment

Awareness of student group dynamics   Some tutors refuse to become involved in any problems that happen in student group work. However, tutors may be unaware of any problems within the groups and may just not be available to be asked for help. In some student situations, tutor intervention may be needed to make sure that everyone in the group works well together. Knowledge of group dynamics can be useful to tutors for several reasons. They could use this knowledge to: choose which students work together on future presentations, change the requirements of the presentation, or just manage them in a different way to reduce further problems. We discuss group work in Chapter 4.

Deeper knowledge of individual students   In lectures, it is usually difficult for tutors to get to know individual students. However, in student presentations, potential leaders in the student group can be identified, as can those students who are less willing to make a contribution in class situations. Working for presentations can help tutors get to know the students as individuals and you may use this opportunity to be more visible in a smaller group of students than lost and unrecognizable in a larger cohort. At some time in the future the tutor may need to provide a reference for you and it is often through work for presentations that a tutor gets to know the students much better.

New knowledge and finding out what students know   As tutors, we have learned a lot from our own students' presentations. For a tutor, there is real benefit in seeing what students have learned, how they approach the topic and present their content to the student audience. The examples chosen and amount of research undertaken can help tutors identify possible gaps in student knowledge or a wider lack of understanding of important principles. If this happens, the tutor can review the topic or create additional handouts to improve student understanding. Tutors do not know everything about their subjects so it is also possible that the content of the student presentation will extend the tutor's knowledge. It may also be possible to detect levels of student enthusiasm and engagement with the topic and this may change how it is taught in the future on the course.

Exchanging roles with the student   Another benefit is through a reversal of roles for the tutor and the student. During the presentation, the student is in control, within a structured academic framework. As the student presenter, you are required to demonstrate your ability to use this control effectively and for the benefit of the audience. By contrast, the tutor may take a more passive role, becoming the listener, the learner and a member of the audience. They will become closer to the real experience of the student; the level of factual knowledge provided; the use or lack of examples to develop further understanding of the topic; the way that technology can help or distract from learning. Whilst the tutor does not take the role of the student, they do have to be more passive and concentrate on what is being delivered rather than being active in the delivery, as they are in lectures.

Experiencing the physical learning environment   On a physical level, by sitting in the audience, the tutor can also experience the comfort or discomfort of the teaching room. You are usually more aware of these features in the audience than when you are the lecturer or presenter. These discomforts might include variations in temperature, a lack of fresh air, chairs that are uncomfortable after 10 minutes, inappropriate table heights that cramp the legs or distracting sound from outside of the room. This can be useful to remind the tutor of the normal student experience of the physical learning environment. It can help tutors to continually review their own teaching styles and methods of delivery so that they include more variety and activities in future sessions.

Perhaps the most rewarding benefit for many tutors will be the opportunity to see their students demonstrating knowledge and communication skills that have developed during the course. For many tutors, the ultimate reward is observing the gradual change from inexperienced student to competent or emerging individual.

Employer audience

We include this potential audience because an increasing number of students are being asked to prepare a short presentation as part of a job interview or an interview for an education or training course. Example 6 in Chapter 1 outlines this type of presentation and we discuss doing presentations for interviews in much more detail in Chapter 11. However, we think it is useful here to remind you briefly that the selection panel or interview panel, whatever they are called, are your audience. You will need to consider some of the points that we have discussed earlier in this chapter and throughout the book. For many students, this can be the most demanding and stressful of all the audiences discussed.

The size and type of this audience will vary depending on the organization and the job involved so it is quite difficult to generalize. This audience may be only three or four people but it could also be much larger if you are asked to present to several teams in the organization, representatives of a local council, partners in a firm or an advisory group for a voluntary sector organization. This is a powerful audience because they will be making decisions about your future based on your performance during the presentation as well as the interview. Somehow, during your presentation, you need to convince them you are the best candidate for the job. Excellent communication and presentation skills are essential. Think about the most important points that you need to communicate in a short amount of time. Also, think about how to create a good impression as a strong candidate before you leave the room. You will need to prepare a very strong presentation to increase your chances of success.

Conclusion

We think it is wise not to underestimate the importance of the audience in your presentation but at the same time, try not to let any fear of the audience overwhelm you. Include them in the planning and preparation stages as we suggest. Consider their different roles and what they need to learn from your presentation. Think about what you can give them that helps them in some way that is unique to your situation. Try to make sure that they think spending time listening to your presentation has been worthwhile and we think your audience will appreciate your efforts.

KEY PRINCIPLES FOR UNDERSTANDING YOUR AUDIENCE

1　Think about your audience and their reasons for watching your presentation. This is an important part of your planning and preparation.
2　Create a presentation that is interesting and provides some value for the audience, regardless of their purpose and reasons for being there.
3　Use the insights you have gained from being a student, and watching many presentations, to develop your own presentation skills. Avoid any examples of poor

(Continued)

practice that you have been subjected to and adapt examples of good practice that have inspired your own learning.

4 Accept the fact that the audience will probably make you nervous. Accept their presence and involve them if it is appropriate. They may be supportive even if their role is to assess your performance and offer constructive comments.

5 Use any feedback given by the audience to improve your future presentations.

7 Developing Content and Structure

LEARNING OBJECTIVES

Reading this chapter will help you to:

- effectively research your content
- consider the structure of the presentation from an audience viewpoint
- ensure that your presentation has a beginning, middle and an end
- decide on a memorable way of beginning and ending the presentation
- have choices for the way that you design the structure of your presentation
- feel confident that the audience will be able to clearly understand the content and structure you have chosen

You will already have started collecting information and by now you have a clear sense about the direction that your presentation is going to take. In this chapter we will give you more information about researching your content and then how to structure your presentation for maximum impact.

Researching your content

You should already have some ideas on how to go about this from Chapter 5. In addition, you have probably got your own way of researching content because you will have written essays or reports for several years now. But there are other ways you may not have discovered which can help you to look for and organize your content. Here are some suggestions.

Finding your way through the literature

To fill in the gaps in your existing knowledge, you will need to discover new material. You may already have effective skills in doing this. If you have not, there are a number of excellent books on the market that will help you such as Bell (2005), Cottrell (2003) or Denscombe (2003). We are not going to give you detailed advice about using keywords or literature searching. Hopefully you will already have this information. Instead, here are some quick but rigorous ways of researching your content.

Use your library   You may have access to a public or an academic library. Even better, you may be a member of an academic library with subject librarians who can provide guidance on resources in your subject area. Some of those resources will be quite general, such as encyclopaedias, and others will be very specific, for instance electronic journals. Explore your own academic library and take advantage of the expertise of your librarian. He or she will be able to offer you ideas on using keywords and the most reliable sources to research.

If you have to work on your own, start by using encyclopaedias and then find introductory textbooks, to give you a sense of the topic.

Use the web, selectively   In some cases, the best way to start is by looking at an encyclopaedia, and if you have access, an electronic encyclopaedia such as Encyclopedia Brittanica, or Wikipedia (Wikipedia, 2007). The latter reference work consists of entries produced by scholars, academics and members of the public. It is very valuable only as a useful starting point. NEVER treat it as the final authority on your topic. There are many other electronic reference sources, as we will shortly see.

Other useful websites include BUBL, which is a UK-based series of links to resources on many topics (BUBL, 2007). Another useful site with a strong US bias is Librarians' Internet Index (LII, 2007).

You might also try the free information available on large academic library sites. Look for appropriate domains, i.e. geographical areas. For instance you can find US educational sites with the domain edu and UK universities with the domain ac.uk.

Use search engines   You may try Google or one of the other major search engines such as Yahoo! MSN Search, Ask or Exalead. You will have noticed that we have not mentioned these as a starting point. The reason is that although these search engines contain a great deal of information, they may not be directly relevant to you, may not be at the right level and may often be downright misleading. There is of course a very useful place for search engine research but it requires experience and care. For some academic topics, you might be better using a search engine with an academic content such as Google Scholar.

Use subject gateways   These are collections of specialist resources which have been collected and reviewed by experts. A good place to start would be the UK Resource Development Network by going to the Pinakes site (Pinakes, 2007). This is a major source of information covering more than 50 subjects.

Journals   These can be extremely helpful but beware of getting too bogged down in complicated topics which are not sufficiently focused on your presentation. Journal articles which take you in too deep and too quickly can be major time wasters!

Electronic journals   These are a particular benefit because you can look at the article directly without having to chase off to the library or send off for it. However the articles are quite often more specific than you actually need, especially at undergraduate level. Again, do not allow yourself to be sidetracked. It is also extremely frustrating to track down an electronic journal and then discover that it is not available locally.

Indexing services   If you really need to get inside your topic at an advanced level, there are many specialist international indexing services available through the web in your library. These will help you to select articles, conference papers, etc. on your topic. Examples would be, *ABI/Inform* in management, *Art Full Text* in art and design, and *CINAHL* in nursing. Some of these services are quite difficult to use. Sometimes you can only see a summary and the full text will have to be borrowed from elsewhere. If you have one, we strongly advise you to consult the subject librarian in your academic library.

PowerPoint presentations   Occasionally you may find a PowerPoint presentation on the web which gives you useful background information. For instance, there may be something provided by a government department. But beware of plagiarism (see Appendix 2).

Collect examples as you research

As you read the literature, remember to collect appropriate examples, case studies, experiments, what worked and what did not.

Learn from your friends

Do you have any friends who know about the topic and could advise you? You may be lucky but do remember that this is only a sensible move when you have developed ideas of your own and have begun to understand the content. If you ask friends too early in your research, you could end up with some very strange and unbalanced ideas!

Creating an effective structure

By now you should have a good idea of your content. Before you start putting together your structure, it is best to stand back a little and clarify a few points. You will find that you can easily and simply put the presentation together if you spent time in advance thinking through the key issues – see Chapter 5. Writing down your structure is just one stage in the process and lots of work needs to be done before you finalize the work.

Before you do anything else, remind yourself again what the presentation is about in one sentence. If you are not clear what it is about, don't expect anyone else to be!

The audience

There is much useful material about audiences in Chapter 6. We suggest that before you continue, you refresh your memory about the nature of your audience. Analysing your audience will help you make the necessary decisions about what you will write. A detailed awareness of your audience will help you to adjust how you develop your material. If you like working with a structured approach, you might want to develop an audience profile, to gain specific information about how the audience might understand and react towards your topic.

So what kind of questions do you to ask yourself?

1 Who is my audience?

- Who is my audience?
- What academic level?
- What purpose will this presentation serve for the audience?

2 What will they want from the presentation?
You may well want to distinguish between what a tutor will want, and what the rest of your student group will want.

3 What do I personally want for myself from the presentation?

- How much does the mark matter?
- Do I feel really serious about this presentation?
- What can I learn from this particular presentation?

4 What, if anything, is bothering me about the presentation?
   For instance:

   - am I concerned about the tutor being too critical?
   - is there enough time to prepare?
   - am I worried about looking foolish in public?

5 What are the positives?
   What are the benefits that I can gain from doing this presentation well?
   With this background information and understanding, start developing the structure.

Developing the structure

Five key points about developing your structure

1 Helping your audience to remember.

   - Psychologists have demonstrated that people are more likely to remember facts from the early part of a conversation or event (the Primacy Effect). So make sure you place a few key facts near the beginning.
   - We remember what we consider to be important, so make sure that you repeat and emphasize key points.
   - Visual aids can be very useful as prompts, either in the presentation or afterwards. Visual aids will help the audience remember and will reinforce your message. See Chapter 8.
   - People also tend to remember what happened at the end of an event (the Recency Effect). So make sure that you have some key points at the end of the presentation.

2 Helping your audience to understand meaning through structure.
   Information has more meaning and is easier to understand when it is structured and sequenced appropriately. Ensure that you have a clear structure that the audience can follow. That structure will very much depend on the brief that you have been given by your tutor.

3 Involve the audience.
   If you want your audience to remember, and benefit from the presentation, involve them in some way. Rather than just telling them, involve them and get their contributions. That way, everybody learns from your presentation.

4 How much is enough?
   As we saw in Chapter 5, it is important to give your audience enough but not too much of a good thing.

5   Be creative in developing your structure.

You have a job to do. You have researched the content and prepared some notes and some ideas. But how are you going to make sense of it all? Develop a clear structure. When you are putting your ideas together, the structure might be displayed in a variety of different ways:

- a sheet of paper
- a set of cards
- a word processed file
- PowerPoint slides
- a mind map
- a storyboard (a series of notes, sketches or visuals planning out ideas and illustrating stages in a production)
- computer software such as MindGenius (2007)

It often does not matter which format you use, providing that you are happy with its organization. You need your own way of developing a clear structure that is evident to your audience. It helps if you enjoy creating it!

Visual aids such as PowerPoint or a flipchart can be extremely helpful in notifying the audience of your structure. We are going to discuss ways of organizing the structure and then look at specific examples that you can use.

Organizing the structure

Now let us look at the three sections of the structure. However you organize the structure you will have:

- the opening
- the middle
- the ending

We are going to consider the way in which you might structure the opening. Then we will look at different ways of structuring the presentation. We then come back to consider the ending.

The opening

There is not a fixed format for the opening. However you have got to give information and also attract the audience's attention.

Welcome and introduction   Cut through any nerves by saying something at an early stage. A few words of welcome may be sufficient.

Say who you are and why you are there   This is often forgotten but it is important to introduce yourself even if your audience knows who you are. It is a useful formality.

Give the presentation a title and say why you are doing it   Apart from anything else, it is important to establish that you and your audience have the same expectations and that everyone is in the correct room!

Mention anything else that is significant   For instance:

- you will be taking questions at the end, rather than as you go along
- how long the presentation will last
- 'by all means take notes if you want to, but there will be a handout at the end'
- 'all this material is available on the website at ...'

Getting the audience's attention   There are lots of ways of attracting the audience's attention. These will not work for everyone and if you do not feel sufficiently confident, that is okay. Some people can make attention-grabbing entrances work, and instantly engage the audience. In the hands of somebody who is shaking with nerves, an attention-grabbing beginning may not work.

Low-risk strategies that are suitable for anyone to use could include simply having a series of notes and a visual aid that enable you to describe:

- a surprising statistic or
- an overview of what you are going to talk about or
- an explanation of why your audience should be interested in what you have got to say

However, you can produce an effective beginning to the presentation without risking too much. Prepare a short anecdote that is relevant to your presentation. Start the anecdote and at the crucial point, break off. It is perfectly okay to have the anecdote written down on cards or paper, providing you can deliver it in a natural fashion. This will only work if your story genuinely does have a point. But it can completely change the shape of your relationship with your audience at a very early stage because you are setting up expectations, and building bridges with them before you have even started your actual presentation. It has the added advantage that you will have fully warmed up your voice. (You can then return to your anecdote right at the end of your presentation.)

Alternatively, look your audience in the eyes and ask a question 'Before I start, I have a question for you. Last week there was a programme on television about whales. Did anybody see it? You and you, that's good. For those of you who didn't, there's a bit when … '. And you are well away into your presentation.

An additional approach is to find an appropriate cartoon or picture to use as a launching point. You could also consider a video clip or a short sound clip, broadcast from a tape recorder or MP3 player.

If you have the personality to carry it off, you can try something dramatic, such as pulling on a prop such as a hat, something from a magic shop, for instance. Alternatively, try reading out a short quotation, or maybe try starting with a particularly striking image on a PowerPoint slide. Ask the audience what it is. A second slide makes it clear that the first slide was a fine detail from a big and complicated structure. That gives you a way in to talk about the relationship between the one part of the picture and the whole picture.

Similarly, draw something on a flipchart and ask the audience what they think it is. After they've all had a chance to guess, reveal that it is a tiny detail from a much bigger picture. Which leads you want to a point about … and so on!

You could get them to look under their seats and pick up the small pieces of paper that you had hidden there. And in the small pieces of paper they will find … we are sure you understand the principle here.

But all of the above require confidence and experience which will be beyond most first-time presenters. However if you are going to try something dramatic or showy, it MUST ALWAYS have a point that is relevant to the presentation.

We have given you three levels of risk strategy – low-risk strategies suitable for anyone; medium-risk strategies for the more confident, and high-risk strategies fot the ultra-confident student. Go with the risk level that seems appropriate and with which you feel comfortable.

There is not one perfect way to organize your structure; there are lots of different ways. It depends very much on the nature of your assignment briefing.

Organize your structure 1

This structure can be used when the presentation is a similar shape to your assignment. The presentation is shaped using a simple table (see Table 7.1).

Table 7.1 An experimental approach in a science or engineering project

Project report	Oral presentation about your report
Introduction including research question, research aims and objectives	**Part I** Introduction Background
Background Literature review Requirements	Objectives
Design Implementation and testing Evaluation Conclusions – including extent to which aims/objectives met	**Part II** Project planning and development Design implementation and testing
Learning from experience References Appendices	**Part III** Issues arising Recommendations Your questions

Doing this is slightly more complicated than it appears. You have to be able to stand back and look at your project or dissertation from a distance, even though you may have only just finished it. But in any case, many presentations will not fall into this relatively straightforward category. You will often have to present on topics that you do not know that well and where the conclusions may not be at all straightforward. So we are going to examine a number of other ways to structure your material, dependent on circumstances.

Organize your structure 2

The simplest and easiest structure to go for is the classic three-part structure – beginning, middle and end. As Aristotle said: 'A whole is that which has a beginning, the middle and end' ((nd) Aristotle in Wikiquote, 2007).

Beginning   Set the scene, provide the background. Give your name and the title of the presentation. Get their attention. Tell them what you are going to do. The question that you are trying to get them to think about is simply 'Who is this person and what are they telling me?'

Middle   Get into more detail, give an outline and analysis of the topic. The questions that you are trying to answer are 'Where did this happen? When did this happen?'

End   Provide findings or solutions, summarize and conclude. Repeat key messages and provide a resolution. The questions you are trying to answer are: 'What are the key issues? What are the key messages?'

Organize your structure 3

It may not be appropriate for you to use a classic three-part BME approach. There are other kinds of ways that you can use to organize the material, such as:

- Classification. Divide your material into groups with common characteristics.
- Chronology. Divide your material into time periods.
- Cause and effect. Describe how one issue has a direct bearing on another one.
- Narrative. Tell a story, describe events or issues. You might well do this from the point of view of a particular individual. The individual might be a person or, if you are feeling particularly creative, might be an inanimate object. An example here would be a presentation about the life cycle of a building, told from the point of view of its air-conditioning system. This needs careful handling.
- Metaphor. For instance if your presentation is about learning to use e-learning software, you might use swimming metaphors: 'When I first learnt to use the college e-learning software I just felt completely **thrown in the deep end** … later on I **began to surface. Treading water. Swimming from end to end** … Started **my advanced course in life-saving …** ' And so on.

Examples

Scenario 1 – Viva   A Viva is where you present an overview of your research to a panel, then answer some questions at a more detailed level. This will be assessed to earn a percentage of marks that contribute towards your final degree classification. One of the tutors is your Dissertation Tutor. You will probably have been taught by the other tutor who is in the same teaching department as your tutor. The tutors will find that with over 30 final year presentations, the whole event is very time consuming and stressful, so it is essential that your presentation is well planned and delivered at the arranged time. To achieve this, 45 minutes has been allocated for each student presentation. Within this time allocation, the student will need to enter the room and prepare themselves, load any PowerPoint presentation, present the content, answer questions, pack up and leave the room.

You are expected to give a brief outline of the research aims and objectives and the methods used. However, the main part of the presentation should concentrate on the

Table 7.2 Viva presentation

The dissertation layout	Oral presentation about my dissertation on organizational culture	Timing
	My name	2 minutes
	Title of my dissertation	
	Part 1	**5 minutes**
Introduction (Chapter 1)	Introduction to the research	
Research aims and objectives	Including aims/objectives and value of the research	
	Justification and scope	
Methods used (Chapter 2)	Background especially on my case study organization	
	How I undertook the project – methods used	
	Issues arising from methods undertaken	
	Part 2	**10 minutes**
Literature review (Chapter 3)	My results	
	1 literature review	
Data collection (Chapter 4)	2 interviews inside case study organization	
	(provide a few useful quotations)	
	Part 3	**10 minutes**
(Analysis and discussion Chapter 5)	Analysis and discussion	
Conclusions	Conclusions	
Recommendations (Chapter 6)	Recommendations	
	Questions please	**10 minutes**
Bibliography	*Watch out for questions about observation. Did I do it properly?*	
	TOTAL TIMING	37 mins!

results, conclusions and recommendations. Your task should be relatively straightforward because you already have a template, a table, to work with.

Scenario 2 – an individual seminar presentation, using the classic three-part structure of beginning, middle and end You are asked to give a paper to a tutor and

Table 7.3   Beginning, Middle and End

Beginning ⇨	Introduce myself Purpose of presentation Topic
Middle ⇨	Details of the topic Investigation Issues
End ⇨	Summary Conclusions and ways forward

members of your cohort, for a design module. The purpose of the seminar is for you to provide evidence of your research into the topic, demonstrating your level of under-standing. Also, in this situation, you take some responsibility for teaching the other students who attend the seminar. They are expected to understand the content and if possible, apply it elsewhere in the module.

This is 'work in progress'. You are presenting ideas, not presenting a polished and finished product. The assignment is assessed and it makes a 20 per cent contribution towards your final mark.

The content of the slides does not matter. What you should take note of is the beginning, middle and end. See Table 7.3.

Scenario 3 – a group presentation on a topic allocated to the group, taking a chronological approach and using a storyboard   You have two assignments. One is an individual project report on a project management topic. The other one is a group presentation which attracts 50 per cent of the total mark for the module. As a group, you have to design and present a project portfolio about a three-day conference. You have to plan the conference, based on a given theme and provide a portfolio of materials for the audience. The portfolio might include: details of the project team schedules, project diary, progress report, progress chasing tools, conference programme, promotion, accommodation, speakers and so on.

There are four of you in the team and you need to divide up the presentation so you all have some responsibilities. It is up to you whether all of you, or just one of you, presents. You are not being assessed on your presentation skills as such. However, the presentation is a vehicle, and a means to display your knowledge of project management and project organization. Consequently the presentation is an important feature of your assignment.

How do you tackle this? You discuss various ways of organizing your material and you eventually decide to use a chronological approach. You have a beginning, middle and an end, but your basic organization is by time, in the build-up to the event.

Again, the content of the presentation does not matter to you. But, please notice the use of a table to sequence the topic into five acts, with clearly defined roles, timings and images. There is much more information about using storyboards and PowerPoint presentations in Cliff Atkinson's helpful book (Atkinson, 2005).

In addition to the basic structure that you have planned, you also need to build in some links. These are normally of two kinds: verbal and visual. Verbal links could include such phrases as 'And now we are going to look at … '; 'The next idea can be tackled in two different ways'; or 'I just want to summarize the three key issues here'. What you will be doing is preparing your audience for what comes next.

Alternatively, you can use your visual aids to create links and bridges between different parts of the presentation using such features as colour, the size and style of the type that you use on your visual aids, and white space. There is much more about this in Chapter 8.

You may very well be asked questions. Questions can greatly clarify what you have got to say. But, if you are not experienced, questions in the middle of the presentation can sometimes unsettle you. So ask for any questions at the end of the presentation. See Chapter 6 for some suggestions for handling questions.

The ending

The ending should bring together what has gone before and develop naturally from it. It is not just a summing up of what you've said; it identifies key issues and links together the main points. The tone is very important. So you might be:

* making key points
* making recommendations

Table 7.4 Storyboard

Topic	Background	Making progress	Preparing for the conference	On the day	Issues arising	Ending
	Project team objectives, planning	Develop materials Key decisions Tools	Quality issues Progress reports Communications	Delivery of materials to audience	Timing What we couldn't control Risk management	Key phrase
Presenter	Joe	Terri-Ann	Alison	Garry	Joe	Alison
Timing	1300	1305	1315	1325	1335	1345
Medium	PowerPoint	PowerPoint Examples of planning tools	PowerPoint (*Emphasize quality costs!*)	Website Folders of materials Style!	PowerPoint	Verbal
Key image	*Team photo*	*Progress chasing*	*Quality and communications*	*Materials*	*Risk management checklist*	*Team photo*

- suggesting a solution
- suggesting a way forward

This is one part of the presentation where it is really useful to have something written down because you may be tired by this stage. We suggest that you have some phrases to hand such as:

> *At this point I want to remind you that there is a handout/website and you will see I have given you key headings and guided reading. I particularly recommend that you look at …*

> *Thanks very much for your attention. I've really enjoyed this presentation and hope you've all learnt something from it. I found it really useful and particularly enjoyed learning something about …*

It's great to end on a joke, if it is something that you can do naturally. But don't force it! It is better to end with a smile than an unfunny joke. If you are in a large group it is possible that your tutor may not have written down your name or student number. Consequently, by repeating your name or ensuring that it is placed on a handout or a PowerPoint slide, you will make sure that the audience, and more importantly your tutor, know your name. This is of course particularly important if you are hoping for a reasonable grade!

Music   You can always finish on either a gentle note or, more lively, if appropriate, by the use of music from a tape recorder, radio or MP3 player. See Chapter 8.

KEY PRINCIPLES FOR DEVELOPING YOUR STRUCTURE

1   Develop an effective strategy to research your content.
2   Select examples as you go.
3   Be very clear about what the presentation is about.
4   Choose the best way to organize the structure for your audience.
5   Ensure that there are sufficient links between the sections.
6   Ensure that you have a strong ending.

Further reading

Aristotle (nd) in Wikiquote (2007) Wikiquote Homepage: http://en.wikiquote.org/wiki/Main_Page

Atkinson, Cliff (2005) 'Setting the stage for your story in Act One', Chapter 2 in *Beyond Bullet Points.* Microsoft Press.

Bell, Judith (2005) *Doing your Research Project*, 4th edn. Milton Keynes: Open University.

BUBL (2007) Homepage: http://en.wikipedia.org/wiki/BUBL.

Buzan, Tony (2003) *The Mind Map Book – Radiant Thinking.* London: BBC Active.

Cottrell, Stella (2003) *Study Skills Handbook*, 2nd edn. Basingstoke: Palgrave Macmillan.

Denscombe, Martyn (2003) *The Good Research Guide,* 2nd edn. Milton Keynes: Open University.

Inspiration (2006) Homepage: http://www.inspiration.com

Librarians' Internet Index (2007) Homepage: http://lii.org

MindGenius (2007) Homepage: http://www.mindgenius.com

Pinakes (2007) Homepage: http://www.hw.ac.uk/libwww/irn/pinakes/pinakes.html

Wikipedia (2007) Homepage: http://en.wikipedia.org/wiki/Main_Page

8 Creating Audiovisual Aids and Handouts

LEARNING OBJECTIVES

Reading this chapter will help you to:

- decide which audio or visual aids will most enhance your presentation
- use audio and visual aids creatively
- ensure that you are properly prepared and rehearsed
- ensure that your presentations are always readable
- minimize the risks when using technological aids

This chapter covers a range of different materials so we have included a listing of key headings:

- **What do we mean by audiovisual aids?**
- **Audio aids**
- **Visual aids**
- **What kind of visual aids?**
- **How do I choose the best visual aids?**
- **Tips on preparing your paper copy visual aids – handouts, notes**
- **Tips on preparing your written visual aids – chalkboard, whiteboard, flipchart**
- **Tips on using artefacts, 3D objects and real life materials**
- **Tips on preparing your projected visual aids – films, slides, videos and DVDs**
- **Tips on preparing your projected visual aids – overhead projector transparencies or slides**
- **Tips on creating electronic presentations – screenshots, live websites, computer software, electronic white boards**
- **Making presentations readable**
- **Key principles for organized audiovisual aids**

What do we mean by audiovisual aids?

In this chapter, we are going to look at different ways in which you can make your presentation more effective by supporting it with different kinds of materials. PowerPoint is such an important communication tool in presentations, that we devote Chapter 9 to it. But we urge you to consider PowerPoint in relation to alternatives. If you want to know more about visual aids, read Chapter 9. In this chapter, we will focus on the general issues of selecting appropriate audiovisual aids and support documentation.

Audiovisual aids and support documentation may include:

- material circulated to the group e.g. handouts
- overhead projector transparencies
- slides
- videos/DVDs
- graphs and charts
- use of chalkboard, whiteboard or flipchart
- electronic information, for example screenshots, computer software, websites or electronic white boards

All these different kinds of supporting materials are referred to in this chapter as visual aids. We refer to audiovisual aids because we will also make a few references to specifically audio materials – sound sources such as tape recordings or MP3 recordings. These under-used resources can also help you to emphasize your points. Table 8.1 shows some different sound sources.

Audio aids

Table 8.1   Audio aids

Type of supporting sound source	Level of sophistication and complexity
Radio	Very simple, low-tech
Tape recording	Very simple, low-tech
CD recording, including both music and other sounds	Very simple, high-tech
Recording onto MP3 player	More high-tech but not too tricky
Sound file on your PC or laptop	Very high-tech, requires technical reliability

You are likely to use a sound source either at the beginning or the end of your presentation. You will probably use it in one of two ways:

1   to liven up the audience and create a sense of anticipation and drama.
2   to calm the audience down by creating a sense of relaxation, and a soothing back-ground atmosphere.

Perhaps the main issues to be aware of are those of age differences and cultural differences. If you choose to start with a lively sample of current pop music, it might work a lot better for peers than for your tutor. Similarly if you have an audience from a variety of cultures, some of them will be much more aware of the cultural significance of your musical choice than others. In general, you might be better to go for timeless sounds. In Western culture, this might be Baroque music, the sound of water or the sea, rather than anything with a very modern feel. As ever, much will depend on your audience.

Visual aids

Visual aids can form a key part of your presentation. They can:

* support what you say – they back up your verbal points with visuals
* add interest to what you say – for instance by providing colour
* explain something visually that would take hundreds of words to explain in text

Example: explaining visually through a Gannt chart   This is a planning and scheduling chart. Imagine how difficult it would be to provide this information through text alone. See Table 8.2 (page 106).

Similarly, visuals can explain some things which are almost impossible to explain in words, for instance organizational charts. See Figure 8.1 (page 106).

Visuals can:

* add humour
* make your presentation much more memorable
* make your presentation much more varied
* make your presentation more fun for all involved!

We want to emphasize the visual aspect of your presentation very strongly. When you stand up and talk, your audience will remember some of what you say. When you stand up and talk *and also* use some kind of visual backup, they will remember more. It is absolutely true that many people have a strong visual sense and that visual information can have a high impact.

Table 8.2 Gannt chart

Week commencing	1–5 Aug	8–12 Aug	15–19 Aug	22–26 Aug	29 Aug–2 Sep	5–9 Sep	12–16 Sep	19–23 Sep
Stages of information audit								
Planning		▓						
Data collection			▓	▓				
Data analysis					▓	▓		
Evaluation							▓	▓
Communicating recommendations								
Implementing recommendations								
Continuum								

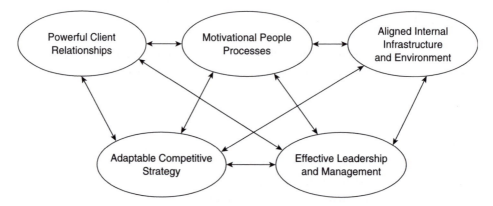

Figure 8.1 An organizational chart

There is also a link to the issue of learning styles. Some of your audience will like learning visually, and they are going to learn much more from a visual presentation than they are from a 'talking head'. See Chapter 10 for more on the concept of learning styles.

Unfortunately, visuals do have a downside. They can:

- overcomplicate if there are too many confusing images
- distract
- make the presentation too long
- give you, the presenter, a lot of stress whilst you develop them!

What kind of visual aids?

There are many different ways in which you can support your basic presentation. Some of these are very high-tech, and some aids can be incredibly low-tech. You must assess what skills you have, how confident you are, and as ever, the needs of your audience.

Whatever kind of visual aids you are going to use, you will need to structure them effectively. You might consider mind mapping to help you develop an appropriate structure. You will find more about mind mapping in Chapter 5.

In addition, whatever kind of visual aids you use, you must make the structure clear to the audience. Think about having an introductory slide/flipchart sheet to explain to your audience the overall shape of your visual presentation. This is very easy to do in a presentation package such as PowerPoint (see Chapter 9). These can either be used individually or of course in combination.

How do I choose the best visual aids?

Is the point of the visual aid to:

- provide background material?
- explain something complicated in a visual fashion?
- emphasize key points?
- provide a visual focus?

Many students and even professional presenters forget just why they are using visual aids. Before you start preparing, make sure you know exactly why you have decided to use some kind of visual support for your presentation. You could use a table like Table 8.3.

Tips on preparing your paper copy visual aids – handouts, notes

Produce material that is legible, that is easy to read, material that has a point, and material that your audience will want to take away – and not throw in the nearest bin! So ask yourself a few questions.

Table 8.3 Types of visual aids and supporting documentation

Type of visual aids and supporting documentation	Level of sophistication and complexity
Notes for your audience Full text of your presentation 'Gapped handout' – audience has to fill in blanks Newspaper cuttings Photocopied set of your slide show	Very simple, low-tech
Flipchart Chalkboard, whiteboard Pointer (for pointing at board)	Low-tech and spontaneous
Slides	More high-tech. Usually requires support
Video, film DVD Overhead projector transparencies	
Electronic slide show, e.g. PowerPoint Electronic laser pointer (for pointing at screen) Electronic displays e.g. screenshots Electronic display e.g. website, software demonstrations, electronic smart boards	High-tech. Sophisticated, complex, but plenty can go wrong! Requires lots of planning.

Question 1   What exactly are you trying to achieve?   Maybe you want your audience to be able to take something away to refer to, or to read afterwards. If you were given this handout in a session, what would you do with it? Most students will use handouts as an aid to recall, scribbling down a few notes and underlining or highlighting as they go along. Sometimes, you may wish to include additional, essential information that you will not have time to cover in the presentation. Your audience can then follow up if they wish.

Question 2   When are you going to use your aids?   You will need to decide if it is best to use them:

- at the beginning of the presentation, to set the scene.
- in the middle, to create a break. For instance, you might want to involve the audience during a presentation, by getting them to fill in gaps you have left in the handout.
- at the end. You might want to hand out additional references, a summary of key points, or a photocopy of overhead transparencies.

Table 8.4   Which visual aid?

Which visual aid?	Why am I using it?	When?	What do I want my audience to do with it?
1.			
2.			
3.			
4.			

You have to decide what you are using the handouts for, when you are going to distribute them and what you expect your audience to do with the handouts. Timing is very important. If you issue your handouts at the beginning, do not be surprised when most of the group spend the first five minutes idly scanning your notes instead of watching you!

Question 3   How do you want your audience to use the aids? What do you expect the group to do with your handout? Do you want them to write on it, read it, file it away and never look at it again? Think about the presentation from the audience's viewpoint. See Table 8.4 above.

Design of paper copy visual aids – handouts, notes

There are a few golden rules which we would encourage you to follow:

- Type or word-process the handouts, or if necessary write out very neatly by hand.
- Select a few well chosen points or provide a summary of the structure of your presentation.
- Don't give the audience masses of paper for no good reason. If there is more than one page, number the pages clearly, so that you can refer to them. Handwritten page numbers are much better than no page numbers.
- Consider 'gapped handouts', in which you provide most of the information but leave a few gaps for your audience to fill in. These can be used to make connections between you and your audience, and provide an activity for them to do.
- Consider a professional looking cover page with your name, the title of the presentation and even a copyright symbol © for added authority.
- Illustrations can be helpful, but remember the laws of copyright. (See Appendix 2.)

There are other tips which are relevant both to flipcharts, whiteboards and to other electronic displays. To see these additional tips, see Making Presentations Readable on pages 115–17.

Is it best to issue the material in a pack or as individual handouts? There are pros and cons. Giving the audience a pack puts all the material together in one place and is easy to manage. Preparing individual handouts mean that you can control the pace of the session and use handouts at the most effective time. As we have already mentioned, this will ensure that the group is not sitting there staring at the handouts, instead of watching you! If you opt to prepare individual handouts, remember to make a note for yourself of when to give them out.

Summary of paper copy visual aids.   Relatively cheap reproduction costs. You are also giving the audience something to take away. However, handouts are surprisingly difficult to get right, and can easily look shabby if you don't take real care.

Tips on preparing your written visual aids – chalkboard, whiteboard, flipchart

Time for our three questions again:

Question 1   What exactly are you trying to achieve?   You might write down a few key points during a presentation just for emphasis. You might ask members of the group to write comments on a flipchart then tear off as individual sheets and fix them to a wall. But this requires confidence and assumes that there will be some useful comments.

It is much more likely that you will either use a whiteboard or a flipchart to prepare some material in advance that you can refer to during the course of the presentation. That is where the flipchart gives you an advantage because you can prepare material well in advance, hide it, and then 'reveal' your surprise during the presentation, by pulling down the top sheet, to reveal your carefully prepared examples. As well as the element of surprise, it means that you can prepare to a high standard. It is also a cheap method of enhancing your presentation and is satisfyingly low-tech; not much to go wrong!

Question 2   When are you going to use your aids?   Probably during the presentation, or at the end.

Question 3   How do you want your audience to use the aids?   You will probably want your audience to take notes from the flipchart/whiteboard or you might just want to add sparkle and a little extra interest to the presentation. For instance, you can turn to the flipchart at the end, flip up a page and say: 'and so in conclusion, to quote Albert Einstein … '. You can then insert your own favourite Einstein quotation.

Ways to create readable flipcharts and whiteboards

Commonsense tells you that you need to write large and write neatly. To find out if what you were writing looks good, try going to the back of the room, and seeing how it looks from there. Can you read it? If not, rewrite it.

If you want your audience to see everything that you have written, you can only use a flipchart or whiteboard in a group of about up to 15 or so. Do think about 'sightlines'. In other words, make sure that all of your audience can see the writing on the board without heads getting in the way. There is more about sightlines in Chapter 10.

Use an appropriate water-based pen. Please remember that some marker pens have permanent ink; okay for flipcharts, a disaster on whiteboards!

Colour is an important issue. See the section on Making Presentations Readable on pages 115–17.

If you have used several flipchart sheets, consider using a big 'thumb tab' to mark each page – in other words a piece of cardboard or paper stuck to the bottom of your flipchart sheet, which acts as a divider. Alternatively, number each sheet separately. It is easy to get in a panic in the heat of the presentation and simply fail to find the page that you want.

Potential problems

Make sure that a whiteboard or flipchart will be available. Always make sure that you have plenty of pens with you, and keep the caps on when they are not in use. Make sure the whiteboard is cleaned before you start.

Summary of flipcharts and whiteboards. Relatively cheap reproduction costs, although the audience gets nothing to take away. One advantage of flipcharts is that you can have a record of main points made in the group; low-tech and effective if your handwriting is readable!

Tips on using artefacts, 3D objects and real life materials

This includes sculpture, paintings, tools, designs, fabrications, medical instruments and so on. In some subject areas, you may be asked to demonstrate a particular technique with a tool or instrument, or you might want to talk about something that you have made yourself. These can illuminate your presentation. You will need to think very carefully about how you are going to use the material and how long you are going to have it on display. It can get in the way of an oral presentation so you may want to use your material for a short period of time, but give an oral presentation separately. Be careful when allowing your precious material to be passed round!

Tips on preparing your projected visual aids – films, slides, videos and DVDs

The technological challenges will be different depending on the equipment that you are using, so here are just a few comments that are relevant to everyone using this kind of technology. You are probably going to illustrate your presentation by using slides, video or DVD clips to illustrate certain points. You really must prepare carefully in advance. That means:

- selecting your illustration with great care
- ensuring that you only need show exactly the material that you want to. To do this, scan the DVD on the day, or check the counter on the video to make sure you can go straight to the right place
- being knowledgeable about how to use the technology
- practising in advance so you know you can handle the technology without getting flustered.

Summary Slides, video and DVDs can be very effective if you are clear about why you are showing images or extracts, and if you are totally sure of the technology. It is really important to ensure that slides do not get stuck and that the DVD always plays.

Tips on preparing your projected visual aids – overhead projector transparencies or slides

You may want to use acetate slides, that is, transparent plastic sheets, and write on them with a pen. Or you might be printing from a word processor or spreadsheet file (such as Word or Excel) onto an acetate sheet. Another alternative is to photocopy onto acetate. The means of production dictates the type of acetate sheets you can use. Acetates for printing on are usually the most expensive.

Question 1 What exactly are you trying to achieve? You will probably be summarizing key points. You may also want to use images such as charts and graphs that you make in Excel and then print out on acetate slides.

Question 2 When are you going to use your aids? It is very common to use overhead projector slides to structure a presentation. So you may want to use your slides all the way through. Alternatively, you can use them at certain points in your presentation, for instance at the beginning, middle, and end. What you must avoid is putting your slides on the machine mechanically and displaying them like a robot! Acetate slides are a visual aid, never an end in themselves.

Question 3 How do you want your audience to use the aids? You will probably want your audience to take notes, be entertained, and to be reminded of the structure of your presentation. There is more on this in Chapter 6.

Readability: ways to create overhead projector acetate slides

- If you are printing from a computer onto acetate sheets make sure that the type is the right size – minimum 24 point.
- Restrict the number of words. Acetate slides will not take many words, so use keywords.
- Use landscape rather than portrait shape, in order to get better visibility on the overhead projector.
- Consider using a neutral slide as a 'screensaver'. In other words, when you want to move away from the words or image projected onto the screen, just put up a neutral slide with a soothing image or the title of the presentation on it. This saves you from constantly switching the projector on and off.
- Consider using a cream sheet of paper as a background (for more on colour see Making Presentations Readable, pages 115–17).
- Consider numbering slides to keep them in sequence.
- Will there be a facility for dimming the lights? This may be necessary to optimize the ability for all to see the screen. If so, nominate someone to act as lighting person.

There are other tips which are relevant both to flipcharts, whiteboards and to other electronic displays. To see these additional tips please see the section on Making Presentations Readable on pages 115–17.

Problems Ensure that you keep the material in the correct order. Consider numbering the slides, and do not drop them! Your audience will have nothing to take away, so it is important that they take notes in the session. Be prepared in case a projector bulb blows. Be ready to ask the tutor for help. It used to be 'the done thing' to switch off the overhead projector when you were not using it, but now it is best to keep the projector on because that protects the expensive projector bulb.

Summary   Producing overhead projector transparency slides, either in word processing software or even by hand, can be highly effective. You can use them to encourage note taking or as a means to provide structure to the presentation.

Tips on creating electronic presentations – screenshots, live websites, computer software, electronic white boards.

Our three questions again:

Question 1 What exactly are you trying to achieve?   You probably want to show examples which are either live or apparently live, for instance web pages, discussion lists or computer software.

Question 2 When are you going to use your aids?   These forms of visual aid are best used when mixed with other kinds of presentation.

Question 3 How do you want your audience to use the aids?   Warning! This point is absolutely essential! Has everyone in the audience got their own monitor? If not, do you want your audience to SEE THE SCREEN? Will you want your audience to take notes, to concentrate in detail on the screen or simply to note down web addresses? If you want them to see what is on the screen in detail, they will probably have to move quite close to it. Is there sufficient space in the room for this to happen? As an example, let us suppose that you want to point out certain buttons on a website. Does your audience really need to see those radio buttons in close-up? If the answer is yes, you probably need a handout as well.

Do not try to demonstrate anything on a projected computer screen unless everyone can see clearly what you want them to see. Do you want to dim or switch off the lights, to get a really sharp screen image, or will your audience want to take notes throughout?

If you are going to use an electronic presentation, you are probably already quite confident in using the technology. However it is worth remembering the following:

- check with your tutor to make sure that everything is set up in advance. Do you have to take responsibility for contacting a technician?
- REHEARSE, because if technology can go wrong, it will!
- get your password issues sorted out in advance.

- ensure that you can access files on the network. Are you able to access the computer in advance and save files to the desktop for a short period? This means that you will not have to hunt around for files or URLs during the demo.
- bear in mind that some software works differently on different computers, and that the setup may be different. For example, different versions of software or some computers may be configured not to accept cookies, meaning access to certain sites is restricted. Always practise in advance on the computer you are using for your presentation.
- similarly, always try to check the sound level on the computer before you start. You want a medium balance so that it is not too soft, but also not blasting out uncomfortably loudly.
- keep your URLs in a separate file, for instance on a USB memory stick or a disk, so that they are there when you need them.
- does the technology need to be live? Would you be able to pre-record your material in advance and play back as screen shots? Check if your department has any software for capturing on-screen images. You could also consider caching websites and saving them to an electronic storage medium.
- will it be possible to dim the lights? If so, nominate someone to act as the lighting person.
- have a back-up position in case the technology fails in the middle of your presentation. For example, consider printing slides onto acetate sheets in advance, just in case.
- your audience may want something to take away. You can always offer to email them a file, or a URL, or provide an annotated handout of URLs. If you are using an electronic whiteboard, you can print out a paper record of the screen content at the time, or download files for e-mailing.

For group presentations you need to be very clear about who is going to be responsible for which part of the presentation. We have more advice on this in Chapter 4.

Problems that might arise include how many people are you expecting and will they be able to attend the session? Are you completely on top of all the technical issues?

Summary Electronic presentations can be highly effective: if you are competent and well rehearsed, if the technology is being used to the full and if the audience can see what they need to see. What will the audience take away?

Presenting numbers effectively

(See Appendix 1 for guidelines on presenting numbers in tables and charts.)

Making presentations readable

Here are six tips which will make your presentations much more readable.

Tip 1 Using type effectively

Typeface Use a conventional typeface such as Times New Roman or Arial. A sans serif font may be more readable for short passages of text. Never use *a fancy type face.*

Capitals Use upper and lower case, NOT JUST CAPITAL LETTERS, which are MORE DIFFICULT TO READ IN A LONG SENTENCE.

Type size Think about an appropriate type size – avoid anything too small when it is projected. If using the projector, 26 point minimum. Make sure it can be seen from the back of the room. Signal the structure using type size. For instance, consider the following for use with an overhead projector:

Point size 26 for major headings

Point size 22 for secondary headings

Bullet points These can be highly effective in moderation. But not page after page!

Tip 2 Structure Have a clear introduction. Describe what you are going to cover. Plan out your main headings, possibly using a mind map or a tree diagram. The structure needs to tell some kind of story, it needs to make sense. Have a clear ending – the ending should have a point to it. Avoid getting too complicated.

Tip 3 Consistent style Retain a consistent style throughout the document.

Tip 4 Colour Use colour carefully and do not overdo it. Generally speaking, avoid more than two or three colours. Red, black, green on white work reasonably well. Avoid light blue, yellow, anything pastel, because you will get insufficient contrast.

Be consistent, for instance, you might want to highlight your main points in green. Then keep to green as the colour for main points. Avoid suddenly switching to another colour. Ensure that you have a purpose in using colour. For example use colours to group themes or points.

If you are going to offer photocopies, ensure that anything that is photocopied works well in black and white.

Colour blindness may be an issue for some people in your audience (10 per cent of men, 0.5 per cent of women). In addition, remember that some of your audience may be dyslexic. The most problematic colours for dyslexics are red and green, followed by blue and yellow. Dyslexic readers may also have problems with black on white and prefer copies on light green or cream paper.

Tip 5 Images   You can greatly enhance your presentation by using images such as diagrams, cartoons, pictures of paintings, and many other kinds of illustrations. See Chapter 9 for where to find images.

Tip 6 Correct your errors before it is too late   Make sure your materials are accurate! If you spell incorrectly, and make basic errors of grammar and punctuation, they will be noticed. It is absolutely essential that you check through your presentation and that you also get somebody else to check it through as well.

If the first slide of your talk is 'Qaulity Management', you have a problem! It is surprisingly easy to misspell keywords, and surprisingly easy to miss them if you just checked it through yourself. It is much more effective to get an independent third-party to act as your quality controller.

You know that lecturers will pounce upon your grammatical and spelling mistakes. This might seem petty to you. However, when you are working in any profession, silly mistakes in presentations get noticed and can harm your reputation.

KEY PRINCIPLES FOR CREATING AUDIOVISUAL AIDS

1   More is less. From the point of view of the audience, too many visual aids do not work. So be highly selective.
2   Be clear about your purpose. Only use visual aids that support your key points. It is a cliché, but it is also true that you are your best visual aid.
3   Be practised. Rehearse with your aids so that you can use them smoothly and confidently. Technical productions often go wrong when they are live; you will be nervous, the equipment can seem unfamiliar. Don't let it trip you up – literally!
4   See and be seen. Make sure that you can see your audience and they can see the screen, the monitor, flipchart or whatever they are looking at. If they cannot see it, for instance because they are too far away, get them closer.
5   Have a backup. Always have a 'Plan B' in case the equipment fails. Imagine the worst that could happen. It probably won't, but be prepared. For instance have some flipchart paper, or sheets of A3 paper and some coloured pens, or an extra set of acetate slides. Ensure that you always have a fallback position.

9 Using PowerPoint Effectively

LEARNING OBJECTIVES

Reading this chapter will help you to:

- avoid the most common mistakes when using PowerPoint, especially avoiding getting too technical
- keep your slides simple
- think about PowerPoint as a component within the overall presentation
- incorporate freely available images into your PowerPoint slides
- know where to look for ideas and inspiration

PowerPoint is presentation software that comes with Microsoft Office. If you have a PC or laptop at home, it will probably be loaded with PowerPoint. The software should also be available on the network in many colleges and universities, because it is the world's leading presentation software. PowerPoint is everywhere! According to Microsoft, PowerPoint is installed on approximately half a billion computers across the world. Think how many individual presentations that might mean per day; think how many individual slides might be generated!

In this chapter, when we refer to PowerPoint, we mean any kind of computer-based presentation software such as PowerPoint, Apple Keynote, open source software such as Impress or web-based presentation packages.

In this chapter we want to give you guidelines on the effective use of PowerPoint. The end of the chapter has some suggestions for what to do when you are having difficulty with a particular PowerPoint problem. We are assuming some basic knowledge of presentation software.

This is a book covering various aspects of student presentation skills and not a book devoted specifically to PowerPoint. Other books talk you through all the standard 'how to' aspects of PowerPoint. They explore all the technical aspects, for instance how PowerPoint can be enhanced through the use of free add-on products such as Microsoft Producer. This chapter is very non-technical.

Background

PowerPoint started out as a graphics program designed by researchers who wanted to find a quick way of presenting information when bidding for research funding. PowerPoint was designed in 1987, and the company which produced it was rapidly bought up by Microsoft. By 2007, PowerPoint totally dominated the world presentation software market, both in commerce and in education.

Most students who are accustomed to using this software will not realize the extent to which it has changed presentations. Only a few years ago visual aids usually consisted of 35mm slides, and hand-drawn acetate sheets projected onto a screen. But now in further and higher education (certainly in the United Kingdom and in the United States), PowerPoint is widely used by teachers as the standard way of presenting. It is also used by students as the principal form of undertaking a class presentation and as a learning tool.

So what's the problem? Most students find PowerPoint fairly easy to use at a simple level. However, its ease-of-use can also be a major problem. It is very easy to make a substandard PowerPoint presentation. Inexperienced users tend to:

- use as many of the features as possible such as lots of exotic fonts

or

- get bogged down in technical complications, because PowerPoint can do lots of very clever things, for example moving text and animations

PowerPoint is capable of producing presentations of great sophistication, with a combination of text images and sound. Therefore it is highly technical. As an example of how complex it can be to understand, the textbook *PowerPoint for Dummies* (Lowe, 2003) is over 300 pages long! Our aim is to help you to use PowerPoint in a simple and easy but effective fashion.

What's wrong with PowerPoint?

The main problem is the way that it is misused. The main charges levelled against PowerPoint by its critics such as the famous academic and designer Edward Tufte (2003: 23) are that it:

- makes presenters lazy and inclined to think in bullet points
- is not good at presenting data because there is not enough space on the slide
- encourages too much reliance on technological gimics such as slide transitions

His criticisms have been taken up across the world by designers and presenters and have led to something of a backlash against PowerPoint. We need to repeat at this point that PowerPoint is an excellent presentation tool, but is easy to misuse.

What is good about PowerPoint?

- It can explain something in visual terms that would take many words to explain.
- It is a comprehensive presentation package. Everything is together in one place: templates, the ability to add sound, colour, to insert graphs and charts, to use images, to link directly with the world wide web. It can also be enhanced by add-ons such as Microsoft Producer, in order to produce dynamic presentations incorporating audio, video, images and web pages. The technology can be used to create potentially astonishing presentations.
- PowerPoint is a wonderful organizer. You can put all your slides in sequence and number them, but you can also edit them and change the order at a press of a button. No-one need ever spill all their slides or acetates on the floor again!
- You can add your own notes to give a personalized commentary on individual slides. You see your notes but no one else does.
- You can run the software as a short automatic presentation while you sit back.

In addition, it can make your presentation much more:

- memorable: through a combination of words, pictures and sounds
- powerful and strong: by using images which impact on the audience
- thought-provoking: by using appropriate quotations and puzzles
- colourful: by making the slides vibrant with background and colourful text
- creative: by designing your own diagrams or by importing photographs, charts, etc (but beware of copyright – see Appendix 2).
- dynamic, current: you can quickly update slides and add new material at the last moment
- fun to create and hopefully to view as well
- portable: provided you know that there is projection equipment available, you can take your presentation around with you on a flash drive. At worst, you can carry a backup copy of PowerPoint transparencies.

Despite all this, PowerPoint presentations are not nearly as effective as they ought to be. Students often put in the effort, but the results are often poor. Why is this?

Mistakes that PowerPoint users commonly make

Content

Too much reliance on PowerPoint   A common mistake with the inexperienced presenter is to rely on PowerPoint too much and to structure the whole presentation around the presentation software. PowerPoint then ceases to be an aid and becomes the total focus. Instead of being a tool, it becomes The Presentation. This often happens when PowerPoint is used as a series of lecture notes which the students simply read out.

Relying on wizards   The Auto Content Wizard can easily lead you down the wrong path, so that you end up with a completely different presentation from the one you intended. You can easily find yourself locked into a style or a way of thinking that does not work for your subject area. For instance, the following slide, based on a template, is attractive, but not a particularly relaxed and gentle way to start thinking about brainstorming. The revised version is easier on the eye. (See Figure 9.1.)

Figure 9.1   Make the slides appropriate

Edit out the detail. Figure 9.2 (page 122) has far too much detail and the audience will find it impossible to read. The alternative on the right is simple and less complicated.

Information overload   Simplify, rather than overload the audience with information. A couple of key points are better than lots of bullet points, as Figure 9.3 (page 122) indicates.

Thinking in bullet points   It is very easy to oversimplify in PowerPoint. Complex ideas in many subjects do not lend themselves to being 'sliced and diced', i.e. neatly packaged into bullet points, as Figure 9.4 (page 123) suggests.

Getting too technical and wasting time 1   Being able to introduce ideas with smooth transitions and sound effects can feel like a tremendous personal achievement. But in doing the technical work, you can easily lose focus and forget key points.

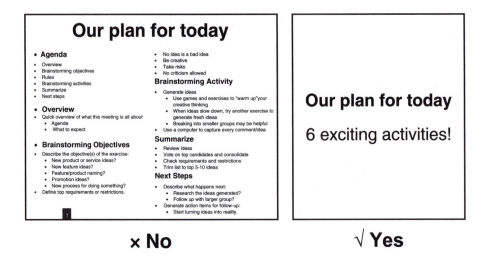

× No   √ Yes

Figure 9.2   Avoid insignificant detail

Getting too technical and wasting time 2   You can use PowerPoint to provide moving images and film clips. You can also use PowerPoint to add a background audio track. However, do consider whether it is worth the effort involved to synchronize the images or audio with your message. If you want to use an audio background:

- think very hard about what will be an appropriate background
- consider using a CD or MP3 player rather than playing the sound file through PowerPoint
- keep asking yourself, if you were a member of the audience, would you enjoy the background sound or might you feel alienated and put off by it?

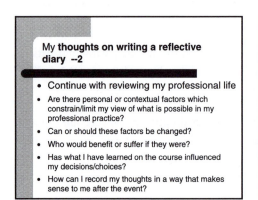

× No   √ Yes

Figure 9.3   Key points

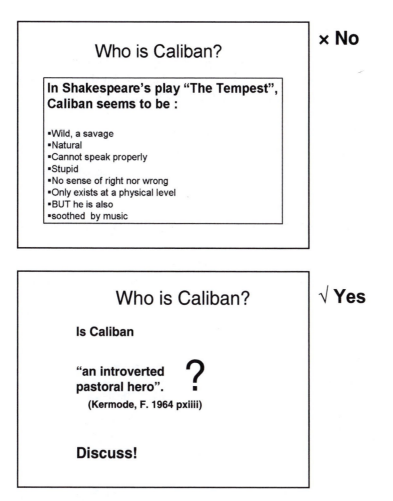

Figure 9.4   Avoid too many bullet points

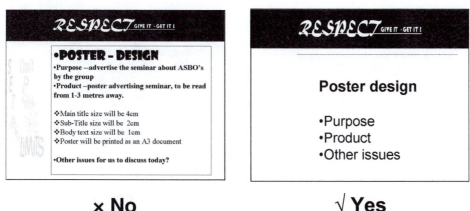

Figure 9.5   Avoid too many styles

How it looks

Too many type styles   The slide in Figure 9.5 (page 123) is confusing because of the range of styles. Stick to plain simple styles. For PowerPoint slides, sans serif styles, i.e. with no tails or curly lines, are preferable to seriffed or curly styles.

Too small type size, making the text unreadable   If you want everyone at the back to see it, 16 point type size is simply not going to work in a medium-size or large room, as you can see from the slide below. Go for a large type size, such as a minimum of 32 point. (See Figure 9.6 below.)

Over complication just because the technology is there   Unnecessary backgrounds, 'water marks', washes and distractions can get in the way and overcomplicate the message. The worst complicating factor is choosing a totally inappropriate and over-complicated type style, as you can see from the following slide. Keep it simple. (See Figure 9.7 below.)

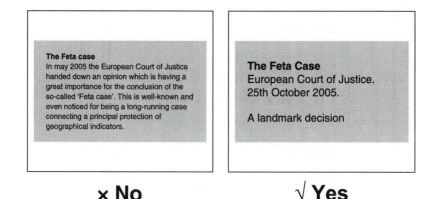

Figure 9.6   Make sure the type is the right size

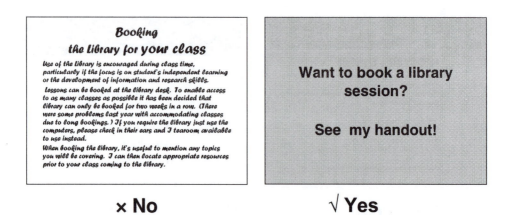

Figure 9.7   Keep it simple

Audience factors

Audiences want variety   Audiences want to see the face, gestures and a human being! They don't want to look at the screen throughout the session.

Audiences can read too!   Don't read out every point on every slide. Please! Most audiences simply do not want you to read it all out. Allow them to read the slide in silence and then maybe ask a question. Do not read out the whole slide and move straight onto the next one. You will simply alienate and bore your audience.

Audiences can snooze   Modern projection equipment is sometimes quite noisy. Audiences can easily be lulled asleep by a whirring noise in the background, a warm room and an endless sequence of slides, especially in the session immediately after lunch.

Audiences can get distracted   PowerPoint was designed for presenting images and simple ideas. It was never designed as a medium for presenting handouts. Audiences may want to look at handouts and a screen at the same time, but the handouts can be a major distraction. The audience may get eyestrain if their eyes have to rapidly flick between long and short distances. They may be tempted to ignore your screen presentations, and idly leaf through their handouts.

If you want your audience to take lots of notes, issue a handout as you start your presentation. If it is not necessary for the audience to take lots of notes, consider telling them that you will provide a set of handouts at the end. The audience can always take notes, and write them up on your PowerPoint handout afterwards.

Figure 9.8   Make your audience think

Introduction	Short automatic PPT presentation	Discussion based on PPT	Verbal Summary	My key point!!	Timing
Flip Chart Quiz!	 Communication skills Issues?	 Communication skills - new skills for today!	Main points = 1. Xxxx 2. Xxxx 3. Xxxx	Handout of PPT image  Communication Skills — Groups and Teams — User Needs — Key Services — Organisational Operations — **Key Factors**	15 minutes exactly!
Time, in minutes					**Total**
2	3	7	2	1	15

Figure 9.9   A draft storyboard

Tips for getting the best out of PowerPoint

1   Think about your audience. What exactly are you trying to achieve? When are you going to use your visual images? How do you want your audience to use the support? Think of PowerPoint as a very useful support. But not as the only resource at your disposal.

Consider what you want the audience to be doing as they see the slides, and afterwards. Thinking? Taking notes? Being entertained?

2   A simple structure for the whole presentation. Do you need PowerPoint for the whole presentation? Think about using PowerPoint as the beginning and ending of your show. Do not structure the whole presentation around PowerPoint. If you start thinking in bullet points, you are probably in trouble!

3   Think in terms of ideas, not bullet points. If you are clear about the ideas that you are trying to communicate, you may find that you can neatly summarize them in bullet points. Or you may find that you need to expand your ideas. You might be better with one PowerPoint slide which you talk about, than half a dozen slides full of bullet points. Figure 9.8 (page 125) provides an idea of how you could effectively and simply open a presentation.

4   Tell a story. If you think of your whole presentation as a narrative, a story, PowerPoint can be a vital part of that story. There is some excellent material on the Web to help you to learn to structure your PowerPoint slides.

By all means, tell a story with a few PowerPoint slides, but remember that PowerPoint software is not the story. It is part of the medium. It is not the message itself. Use it as part of a bigger story in the presentation. For instance you could run a short, three-minute, automatically timed PowerPoint show within your overall presentation, as a short sequence within a longer talk.

5   Use a storyboard. There is some very useful material on the Microsoft site about planning your PowerPoint slides with a storyboard. You could use a storyboard to plan the whole presentation, including the section with PowerPoint. (See Figure 9.9, page 126.)

6   Use images to support the central message. One of the hardest aspects of presenting is to use visual images that reinforce your message rather than detract from it.

The three steps are:

1   finding images to support the text
2   being clear what you want those images to say
3   then using images to help tell the story

Is your image going to complement the text? In other words will it support the text and work with the text. Or will it supplement the text? In other words, will it add something new to the text and elaborate in some way, like the image in Figure 9.10 (page 128)?

7   Keep it simple. The basic layouts and designs in PowerPoint will work if you keep them simple. After all, they have been designed by presentation professionals.

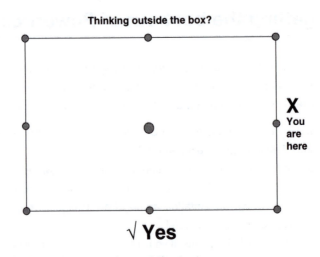

Figure 9.10   An image can supplement the text

So set yourself simple guidelines such as in Table 9.1. See Table 9.1 (page 129).

Some examples of simple but effective slides, using a template design by a student, are shown on page 130.

Diagrams

You can create diagrams yourself by using simple drawing tools within PowerPoint. It is quick and straightforward to create boxes, lines, arrows. An example of this is Figure 9.14 (page 132). Or consider drawing something by hand and scanning it into your computer. What you lose in polished performance, you may gain in spontaneity and creativity. Your tutors will appreciate something that looks a bit different. Sometimes, an object that looks a little less polished can be highly effective, as Figure 9.15 (page 133) illustrates.

Ensure that everyone can see the images that you are using in PowerPoint.

1   Check that your type size is sufficiently large. Probably you will need at least 32 point.
2   Press F5 to show the whole screen.
3   Ensure that you drag pictures right to the corner of the screen so they are as big as possible.
4   You can also use the zoom feature in PowerPoint to focus on a particular issue. For instance, use zoom to highlight one part of an equation, or a detail on a drawing.

Presenting numbers

Only state the most basic headline numbers in PowerPoint slides. If you want to display graphs or charts that you have created, use handouts to get more space. (See Appendix 1.)

Table 9.1   Simple PowerPoint guidelines

Guidelines	Comment
Keep it readable	Do not use any unusual type styles.
Keep it plain	Plain, simple style. Avoid watermarks, fancy backgrounds. Prefer plain sans serif type styles such as Arial or Univers.
Keep a consistent style	Use a very small number of type styles.
Minimize words on the slides	Some experts suggest that 12 words per slide are the absolute maximum. Some would say just six words!
Minimize bullet points	Too many bullet points can get messy, untidy, very tedious and difficult to read.
Use colour sparingly and carefully	Remember that some of your audience may be colour blind.
Avoid movement	Movement can cause distraction and can look unintentionally funny.
Avoid anything that is complicated	Unless you are being assessed on your technical skills, avoid technical complications.

Images for PowerPoint

Let us assume that you may want to put some images in your PowerPoint presentation. You know that there is clipart available on PowerPoint, but you are not inspired by it, and you'd like to find something different. You probably don't want to pay a fee to the provider of the image, so you will want to use a free image. You will also want to do it legally, and of course you will not want to infringe copyright law.

Copyright issues   Clipart that comes with the software will be no problem. However, most images on the web and most images available through data banks are restricted in some way. Any kind of re-use, including in a student project, could potentially break copyright law. In general terms, students can copy material under the fair dealing exception for 'research or private study'. Make sure you are clear about the terms of the copyright holder. Consequently any collection which has already been cleared for copyright, such as a university or college collection of digital images, is going to be very

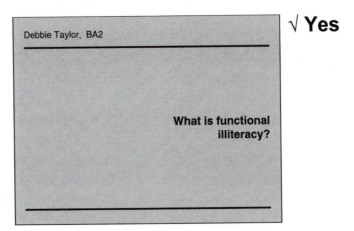

Figure 9.11   Home-made template design slide one

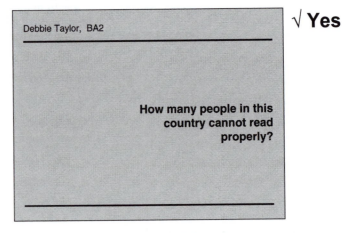

Figure 9.12   Home-made template design slide two

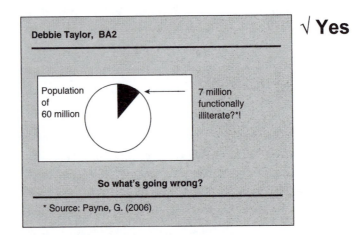

Figure 9.13   Home-made template design slide three

helpful when you are using PowerPoint. Of course, if you make your own images, they are your own intellectual property and you do not need to be concerned about copyright. For anyone concerned about copyright issues, which should be all students, the organization TASI is very helpful in this area – see below.

So where do you go to obtain free images? Here are some suggestions. What is available to you depends on your country, and quite possibly your college and its resources. The following suggestions are primarily for UK students but are relevant to all students.

- Microsoft Office online. Clipart. http://office.microsoft.com/clipart/default.aspx?lc=en-gb (You have to be careful how you use this and you must abide by all their guidelines. However there are lots of images here that go way beyond the clipart available in your standard Microsoft Office package.)
- AHDS visual arts. http://vads.ahds.ac.uk/ (National service sponsored by UK Jisc. Look for the search images button.)
- SCRAN database. http://www.scran.ac.uk/ (This is included as an example of the sort of subscription database that your own library might have. It can only be used for educational purposes but is very useful.)
- TASI (Technical Advisory Service for Images). http://www.tasi.ac.uk (National service sponsored by UK Jisc. A storehouse of material, at a technical and scholarly level. Useful for guidelines on the legal position. In particular, check out the following for finding images online – http://www.tasi.ac.uk/advice/using/finding.html; finding stock images – http://www.tasi.ac.uk/advice/using/finding_stock.html; and a review of image search engines – http://www.tasi.ac.uk/resources/searchengines. html.)

Image searching tools   Many general search engines have an image searching facility, for instance Google or Yahoo images. You can use the advanced search feature to pick up more specific images, for instance, to pick up images specifically from the UK universities search on domain ac.uk. TASI has many more examples of search tools. Do consult this service, because image searching tools are constantly changing and developing.

There are several collections which can be safely considered for educational use. The most well-known of these is Flickr (http://www.flickr.com/). This contains collections of photographs made available for individuals. Some of these are only available to individuals in a closed group, some are available to everyone. Each individual photograph has a copyright and licensing statement making it clear how it can be used. Searching is not particularly straightforward but you can try using the search tools to find freely available materials.

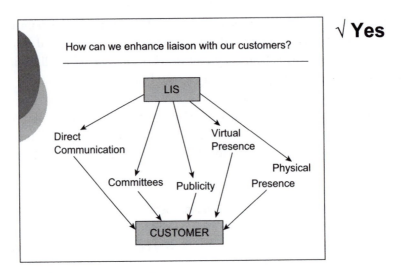

How can we enhance liaison with our customers?

√ **Yes**

Figure 9.14   Design your own charts

The alternative is Morguefile (http://www.morguefile.com/); a morgue file is a newspaper term for an archive of news material, photographs and so on. Morguefile is an international file of high-resolution digital photographs for public use.

The third major database to consider is Wikimedia Commons (http://commons. wikimedia.org/). This is a massive database, part of the Wikipedia project. It contains many images and other kinds of content such as puzzles, diagrams and videos clips. All of these are freely available. You are allowed to copy, display and modify the files but you have to acknowledge the source and the authors. You also have to agree to release any copies or improvements that you make, so that other people may use or add to your work. You are encouraged to contribute your own work – to give as well as to take.

The advantages of this fantastic collection include the fact that a number of major collections are part of the project and are therefore now in the public domain. It is also relatively easy to search. Each file has a brief history, and in some cases, links to other material. More details can be found at: http://commons.wikimedia.org/wiki/Commons: Welcome

Scientific images   Many American federal agencies have scientific images available without copyright restrictions. The best place to investigate these is through TASI: http://www.tasi.ac.uk/advice/using/finding_science.html. This leads to both American sites and extensive resources through the UK Intute academic service.

Digital camera   Last, and certainly not least, if you can get access to a digital camera, then a totally new world of PowerPoint images opens up to you. If you take your own

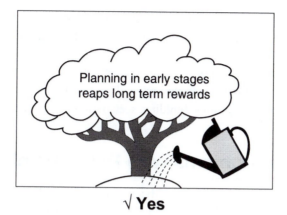

Figure 9.15 **Hand-design your own images**

Figure 9.16 **Use your own photographs**

Figure 9.17 **Be creative, be relevant**

photographs, you will have legal control of the image and you can use your creativity to put across the message that you want. (See Figure 9.16, page 133.)

If you take photographs of people, you must always ask them if they mind you using their image. If the child is a minor, you must always seek parental permission. If you are taking photographs in a public building, seek permission before photographing.

If you have problems with PowerPoint

There are many books which give you advice on using PowerPoint. There is of course a lot of information available within PowerPoint itself, either by using the Office Assistant or by using Microsoft Office Assistance if you are connected to the web. The Microsoft website has many useful tips and guidelines such as the tips on using a storyboard to plan your presentation.

Beyond this, many universities and colleges will have their own guides to using PowerPoint. There may be one in your own institution. Failing that, go to your favourite search engine and use the advanced search function to enter PowerPoint tutorial and domain ac.uk which will get you a list of UK academic PowerPoint tutorials.

KEY PRINCIPLES FOR EFFECTIVE USE OF POWERPOINT

1. Keep reminding yourself that PowerPoint is a support for your presentation, not the presentation itself.
2. Keep thinking from a user perspective, and provide clarity and simplicity plus sufficient information.
3. Use PowerPoint for what it does best – linking text and images.
4. You are not alone; there is a great deal of free support on the web.
5. Stay in charge. Make PowerPoint your trusted servant, not your boss!
6. Enjoy, and express yourself creatively. (See Figure 9.17, page 133.)

Resources

Atkinson, Cliff (no date) *Create a storyboard*. Microsoft office online, available from: http://office.microsoft.com/en-gb/FX011886751033.aspx

Lowe, D (2003) *PowerPoint for Dummies*. USA: J. Wiley.

Tufte, Edward (2003) *The Cognitive Style of PowerPoint*. Connecticut: Graphics Press LLC.

TASI (Technical Advisory Service for Images) (2007) http://www.tasi.ac.uk

10 Learning from Presentations

LEARNING OBJECTIVES

Reading this chapter will help you to:

- appreciate each presentation as a chance to learn something new
- remain interested in how your audience learns
- plan your presentation to take into account different ways of learning
- choose a particular technique to help you learn from your next presentation

You may well have heard the tutor say something like the following: 'Doing a presentation is a very good learning experience. It will benefit you greatly'. How exactly is doing a presentation a good learning experience? Why should you bother to 'learn from your presentation'? Here are some good reasons:

- correcting mistakes. At a basic level, if you do not learn from your mistakes, you will simply keep repeating them next time.
- making improvements. If, however, you can learn from your presentations, you will get more competent each time you have to do a presentation.
- feeling better about presentations. This means that learning from your presentations makes them more enjoyable for you and your audiences.
- gaining satisfaction. There is always room for improvement. However well your presentation goes, you can gain satisfaction by knowing that next time it can be even better.
- improving employment skills. Learning from your presentations is part of a bigger process of learning from experience and developing your employment skills. It is absolutely essential when you undertake presentations for job interviews. See Chapter 11 for more on this.

A good learning experience – what can you learn from your presentation?

It is easy to just forget about a presentation as soon as you finish. It is easy to 'Put that down to experience', and then dismiss it from your mind. But you can learn lots from every presentation that you do. For instance, you can learn:

1 Ways of handling presentations, for instance, specific ways to decide on the choice of visuals. See Chapter 8.
2 How to motivate your audience. You are motivated to do a good presentation. But how can you motivate your audience to enjoy it?
3 How you react under pressure, learning more about your ability to think on your feet in pressurized circumstances. Tutors do not normally show you how to improve your ability to react under pressure; they just assume that you will learn it. See Chapter 3 for our tips.
4 How to correct mistakes and make successful presentations even more successful.
5 How to work with a group when preparing a presentation.

Anyone who has ever done a presentation will have a vague feeling afterwards, either that it went well or that maybe it did not go too well. Later in this chapter, you can learn techniques which will help you to be specific about what worked and what did not.

A good learning experience – how can you help your audience learn from your presentation?

Your presentations will improve if you have some idea of how your audience can learn from your presentation. Learning doesn't just happen. In the last 30 or so years, education researchers have discovered that we don't all learn in the same way.

Tutors now place the emphasis on learning rather than teaching. In your presentations, you are helping your audience to learn. We know that some methods of learning work better for some students than others. Some students enjoy lectures; some students hate them. Some students enjoy learning on a computer, others want face-to-face interaction, not just a computer screen.

This is partly because we learn in very different ways. Here is a practical example. Just imagine yourself in a class where first-year students are being taught how to use the college's computerized virtual learning environment. The students are learning a computer system which is not especially difficult, but is new to all of them.

If you were in that class, looking around you, you might soon notice:

- some students conscientiously taking notes
- a couple of students chatting
- others sketching out a diagram of the virtual learning environment
- some students fiddling with their pencil or pen, keen to get started on the keyboard
- others asking complex theoretical questions about the computer network
- one or two students sitting quietly, eyes closed, maybe dreaming how the parts of the system linked together
- others feeling most comfortable working through the instructions at their own pace, using a workbook

All of the students we have just described are learning; they are just learning in different ways. We all think differently, we will learn differently. Generally speaking, the more we learn, the more we develop our skills to learn.

Different styles of learning

Learning theory is a fast evolving area. What follows are some well-known learning styles. They are not 'true' or exact descriptions and there are lots of others to choose from.

VARK – Visual, Auditory, Read/write, Kinaesthetic learning

The principle here is very simple. We all experience the world in different ways and we are likely to be inclined to use one of our senses more than the others. The following are preferences, however, rather than strengths.

Visual learners   Some of us are highly visual. Visual thinkers need to see visual explanations, for instance using PowerPoint, charts or diagrams. They are very aware of what is going on around them, and the room in which they are learning. They enjoy seeing colours being used, for example, with posters, a flipchart or videos.

Auditory learners   Some of us are auditory, that is, our first reaction is likely to be through our sense of hearing. So we remember sounds, we enjoy having explanations told to us and we react really well to discussion, conversation and certain kinds of background music in the classroom. We often react very badly to external noises such as a noisily flickering neon tube, or a poorly maintained projector.

Read/write learners These thinkers like words. They make lists, they take notes, they underline, and they actually read the handouts! They enjoy working from manuals and work-books. They feel disturbed when they are told that they cannot take notes. When presented with visual representations, they might want to change diagrams into words to make understanding easier.

Kinaesthetic learners Some students are going to be primarily kinaesthetic, that is, they are very physical and aware of their bodies. They might be very fidgety in class and wanting to do things, to move, to touch, to experiment, to learn by doing. They appreciate any kind of tactile activity in the presentation, even if it is just receiving a handout. Kinaesthetic thinkers will not want to sit still for hours at a time without stretching. They may also feel things deeply, and presentations which appeal to their emotions can be highly effective. In practice, many students will have a combination of two or more VARK preferences. Some students will be more adaptable learners than others, but it is likely that we all have a natural preference for one particular style of learning.

Using VARK in your presentations

Try to provide a range of sensations in your presentation

V   Ensure that there is strong, well presented visual content

A   Speak clearly and consider if you can use any kind of background sound sources

R   Ensure that there is something to read – with a small group, a handout, with a bigger group, a few references

K   Ensure that the audience gets some chance to move, unless it is a very short presentation.

Make the presentation multisensory, something that all of your audience can get involved with through their senses.

Importance of a learning environment

Many students and tutors do not put enough emphasis on the physical environment in which we learn. Tutors have a reasonable amount of control over the classroom or lecture theatre; students doing the presentation may not. However, you can make a difference to the room that you are working in, and this difference can help you to create a strong presentation. If you are doing your presentation in a hot stuffy room, with poor lighting and all your audience sitting at the back of the room, it is very hard to be motivated. You can nearly always change some aspects of the environment to improve motivation and learning. What can you change?

Lighting   Make sure that there are no problems with reflections on a projection screen if you are using one. If necessary, switch off some of the lighting but make sure that the group can still see to take notes. If you are lucky enough to have a dimmer switch, consider adjusting it. If there is natural lighting, use it to the full; pull up those blinds unless it is essential to have the room darkened for a projector, or the sun is shining in someone's eyes.

Temperature and air quality   These are obvious, but vitally important. We all learn better with fresh air around us, supplying oxygen to our brain. The brain works better at lower temperatures than it does when overheated. If possible allow some flow of air, for instance by opening a couple of windows just before the presentation.

Sound   We have already discussed the possibility of using sound sources as part of your presentation. You can soothe your audience or liven them up by having an appropriate acoustic background. There is research evidence that in some cultures classical music, such as Mozart and some Baroque music, can increase the length of study times and improve memory and performance.

Space   You may not be able to do much about the physical space in the room. However, is it possible to move the chairs around to create a more interactive learning space? If your audience is sitting on rows of chairs, they cannot see each other and cannot share ideas. If you just want to tell the audience facts, sit them in rows. If you want them to debate and discuss, consider a semi-circle or 'horseshoe' shape. See Figure 10.1. If possible, ensure that your audience has enough space to be comfortable and are not too far apart to be totally isolated from each other. Kinaesthetic learners in particular will appreciate the opportunity to move round a little.

Smell   Our sense of smell is much more important than we sometimes realize. Think about using a scent to encourage your audience to become more mentally alert. For instance, air freshened with a rosemary, lemon or lime smell can encourage mental alertness. Relaxation can be encouraged by such scents as lavender and chamomile. Consider using a little essential oil on tissues or cotton wool distributed about the room.

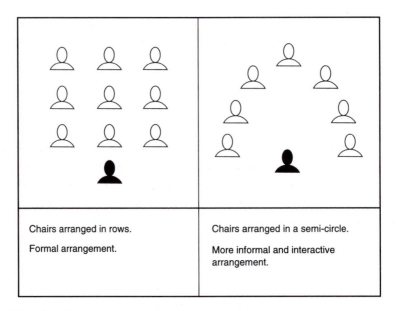

Figure 10.1 Seating arrangements

Water   Our bodies need water to survive and our brains need to be regularly watered. If you are only presenting to a small group, is there any way that you could provide cups of water? Always make sure that you have drunk some water before you start.

Other ways of helping learners' brains to be fully engaged for your session

The BME factor   Every presentation needs a Beginning, a Middle and an End (BME). We learn more successfully at the beginning and at the end of a learning activity than in the middle. Concentration is higher at the beginning than at the end, so aim to create small beginnings and endings within a longer session.

Break it down   If you have followed our advice in Chapters 5 and 7, you will not have too much content. If you are worried about content, break it down into 'chunks' that are easy to understand.

Add stimulus and variety   You can sometimes improve the quality of the sessions by asking your audience to change places, then get up and move around or even to talk to each other. This works well with younger groups but has to be handled carefully with adult learners! Think hard about what you would find acceptable if you were in the audience, rather than standing at the front.

Using the learning environment in your presentations

If possible, try to provide an environment which encourages your audience to learn. Think about such issues as:

- space
- heating
- lighting

Ensure that everybody's brain is engaged in the session.

- Break the session into small chunks
- Provide a variety of experiences

Keep thinking about what it is like to be a member of the audience, and remember the audience's physical and mental needs.

Tell them a story   For some subject disciplines, and for some environments, it might be appropriate to use a story. If you feel confident in front of the group, consider beginning or ending your presentation with a short story. In the last few years, storytelling has been increasingly recognized as an effective way of presenting information to adults in ways that they relate to and remember.

You might want to describe a real event, something that happened to you, or perhaps you may want to use something that you have made up: 'I have just realized why I have been misunderstanding how neural networks are suppose to operate. Last night I was playing with my pet cat when …'

Similarly, you can disguise a true event or make it distanced from you: 'I would just like to tell you a little bit about a friend of mine, who had an interesting insight when he was listening to the BBC's economics correspondent on the radio recently. The correspondent was talking about PFI, and he said that …'

Stories can be:

- comforting – many of your audience may remember storytelling from school
- believable
- entertaining
- memorable

- capable of communicating messages
- funny – if you happen to have a gift for humour!

This can be a high-risk strategy and is only recommended for confident presenters, or those who are prepared to make a recording in advance and then play that to the group.

So what can you do with these strategies to encourage learning?

- Acknowledge that people learn in different ways, therefore your presentation has to offer a variety of experiences.
- Adapt your presentation so that you are not stuck in one particular delivery style. For instance do not get stuck in one physical spot for the whole time, just talking to PowerPoint slides.
- Be flexible in your outlook, because not everyone is going to learn in the same way as you.

How are you going to learn from your own presentation?

Learning before the presentation   Review previous experiences of presentations. Even if you have never done a presentation in your life before reading this book, you will have had experience of presentation as a participant, as part of the audience. So if you were wondering how to start shaping a presentation, you could ask yourself:

> *What is the best presentation I've ever done?/what is the best presentation I have ever seen?*
> *What was it about the presentation that made it the best?*
> *What could I take from the presentation and feed into the one that I've got to do?*
> Ask yourself: *what was the worst presentation I have ever seen?*
> *What was it about the presentation that made it so bad?*
> *What could I take from that poor presentation to ensure that I don't make the same mistakes?*

Learning during a presentation   You are going to be busy during the presentation and you will not have a lot of time to be reflecting on what you are doing. However there is nothing to stop you having a notepad and a pen with you and making a few notes. If anything seems useful, just make a brief note of it at the time. Supposing that you notice that your audience sit at the very back so that the first three rows of seats are totally empty. Make a note to yourself: 'Next time I get here early, and encourage my audience to fill up the first few rows!!' At the end, just collect up your notes with your other materials. You can of course do what some professionals do and use a questionnaire. But we wouldn't advise it for a student presentation. Instead, go for informal feedback, as we will shortly explain.

Learning after the presentation   If you feel sufficiently self-confident, ask your friends in the audience what they thought of it. But looking for praise and confidence boosters will not tell you very much, as in:

Question: Be honest, what you think of my presentation?
Answer: Yes, it was great, really interesting.

Instead, try something like:

Question: What did you think of the presentation? Was there anything specific that you think I could do to improve?

Or

Question: If you could change just one aspect of my presentation, what would it be?

Equally, you could ask the tutor for some feedback at the end. If you are lucky, you will get a positive and thoughtful response. It may not be possible if the presentation is being assessed. Either way, you want to make sure that you get feedback as soon after the presentation as possible – don't leave it for a couple of weeks! Unless your presentation was extraordinarily good or terribly bad, it will not be remembered and your tutor will not be able to give you a detailed level of feedback.

The process for giving yourself feedback can be a bit challenging, especially if things did not work out in the way that you had hoped. Try taking yourself through the presentation again, relive what you did slowly and gently, from scene to scene, using notes that you took at the time, remembering the people there, and how they reacted as the presentation developed.

If you come to any parts of the feedback that you do not feel happy with, run through the part again and try making a few adjustments. For instance, if at one point during the presentation, you nervously drank a glass of water and spilt it down your shirt, just imagine yourself going through the action again, but this time, you pick up the glass very carefully and slowly and thoughtfully sip the water. Practise it a second time in your mind. Only move on when you feel comfortable.

This is like the mental rehearsal exercise we looked at earlier in Chapter 3, only after the event. You can get rid of bad feelings about the presentation. Firstly, issues that seemed large to you at the time will probably not bother all the other participants. Secondly, your audience is almost certain to let go of the presentation very quickly afterwards. You are the only one who is likely to worry! But also, you are the one that can learn the most from it.

However, remember that some parts of the presentation will have gone well. As you run through the scenes again, what aspects of the presentation do you feel happy about? Do your best to visualize those particular parts of the presentation, one by one. Magnify any sound that you remember. If you got a laugh or some smiles, focus on them. Intensify the colours that you can see. Congratulate yourself on doing a really good job and think about what you can learn from this success. What can you take away that you can use elsewhere?

However well or badly you think it went, don't be too hard on yourself. You have just undertaken a presentation; you have not just been responsible for a major surgical procedure! So be kind to yourself, whilst being honest.

A learning log or learning journal   If you want to learn from your presentation, right through from the beginning to the end, consider keeping a learning log. This is really just like a diary, but focused on what happened and what you can learn from it. Use this to deepen the quality of your learning and understand your own learning processes. Here are some example headings:

- The aspect of the recent presentation which I want to learn from is this:
- The specific issue for me was this:
- How I acted at the time:
- How I felt at the time:
- How I felt later on:
- How I might have appeared to others at the time:
- Reflecting back on it now:
- My plan for next time – how I will aim to act/feel next time:
- What I need to do to help me act/feel appropriately next time:
- Specific steps to take:

You can then come back to these learning logs at a later date to review your progress. The most successful way to ensure that you learn how to present information well is to practise, and reflect on your experience. We hope that we have encouraged you to learn from each presentation.

KEY PRINCIPLES TO HELP YOU TO LEARN FROM YOUR PRESENTATION

1   Use each presentation as an opportunity.
2   However good your presentations are, there is always room for improvement.
3   Your audience consists of individuals with different ways of learning, so appeal to different learning styles.
4   Develop specific techniques that will help you to learn from the presentation.

Further reading

Campaign for Learning (2007) Website: http://www.campaign-for-learning.org.uk/aboutyourlearning/whatlearning.htm, accessed September 2006.

Fleming, Neil (2007) *VARK: a guide to learning styles*. Available from: http://www.vark-learn.com/english/index.asp, accessed September 2006.

11 Delivering a Presentation as Part of an Interview

LEARNING OBJECTIVES

Reading this chapter will help you to:

- understand the special nature of this type of presentation
- balance your time effectively between the interview and the presentation
- see the presentation in the wider context of the interview event
- appreciate the different perspectives of interviewer and candidate
- learn from your experiences of delivering these presentations

There is an increasing trend for students being asked to deliver a presentation as part of an interview for a job. These presentations can vary between short, 5-minute presentations on any topic of their own choice to longer presentations of 20 minutes on a given topic relevant to the job. Students have sometimes been asked to identify the most important challenges, or have been given a list of challenges, facing a specific employment sector and are asked to discuss these challenges. Some students have been told they have to use PowerPoint but other students have been told they cannot use any technologies, just their speech and handouts.

You can see from these examples that there are many different presentation types and styles used, each unique to the interview situation. There are, however, several generic principles to the interview presentation and we hope this chapter will help to prepare you for this type of presentation, whatever the job. Before we do this it is useful to think about why presentations are used with job interviews.

Reasons for including presentations as part of the selection process

1 Choosing new staff is an expensive process so any method that helps to make this choice clearer is useful.

2 The wider range of media formats available in society has influenced the increasing importance of the visual performance of candidates.

3 Communication and presentation skills are essential for many jobs. Also, some employees represent their organizations by delivering presentations to people within and outside of their organizations. Assessing presentations is seen as a suitable method for choosing the best candidates for these jobs.

4 Presentations provide additional information about candidates that complements the information given on the application forms.

5 Presentations from candidates can help to generate more specific questions that are different from the general questions asked of all candidates in the interviews. These presentations can be an opportunity to show the personality and individuality of the candidate, compared with other procedures which tend to judge the candidate within a standard framework of criteria.

For most of us, a job interview is a very stressful experience and being asked to deliver a presentation as part of the interview can increase this stress even more. We discussed aspects of this type of audience briefly in Chapter 6 but it is useful in this chapter to be reminded about the special nature of the audience for a presentation in an interview. Whilst this audience could be described as the interview panel, we use the term interview audience as a wider term because in some situations other members of the organization can be invited to watch the presentations of the interview candidates. In these situations the audience is larger than the interview panel.

The interview audience

If you have applied for a job where you have never worked or even visited before, it is very likely that members of your presentation audience will be strangers. They will all be watching to assess you in some way for your suitability for the job or the organization but also, they may each be looking at different aspects of your presentation. Their different roles on the interview panel may or may not be explained to you. However, your presentation will need to impress them enough to convince them that you are a strong candidate for the job.

If you apply for a job in the organization where you currently work, you may know or have already met some members of the audience. These people may not be your friends but will perhaps be colleagues from other departments in the organization. This can make some applicants more nervous than presenting for strangers. With strangers, you will probably never see them again if you are not given the job. With colleagues, you will have to continue working with them in your existing or new role. You might feel embarrassed or awkward about your presentation or the outcomes of the interview if you are not chosen for the job.

For some job presentations, this audience will remain detached, perhaps make brief notes but not interact with you in any way. You might be asked questions by the interview panel at the end of the presentation or they could ask you to leave the room so that the next candidate can present. The format will vary so be prepared to be flexible.

For interview presentations, it is important to remember that the selection processes used for most jobs should filter out the weaker candidates so that only a small number of applicants are interviewed. These final candidates will probably be fairly equal in their suitability for the job. They are likely to share similar qualifications or experience so the presentation can play a very important part in who is chosen for the job. If you are asked to give a presentation as part of your interview, you will need to give an impressive performance to convince the audience you are the best candidate. After all candidates have presented, the interview panel will probably discuss each one in turn so you need to be remembered, to stand out from the others in some memorable and positive way.

For most interview presentations, these audience factors are beyond your control. You have to accept them. What you can do, however, is to turn the situation to your advantage by preparing a really strong and interesting presentation within the guidelines you have been given. Follow the advice and suggestions throughout this book, rehearse your performance, deliver the presentation and then tell yourself that it is over. The decision is made. Reflect on any feedback given, what you thought went well and what could be improved but then move on. If you were not chosen for the job, try to put it down to experience. You will have learned something useful from the interview and presentation that will certainly help you in the future. If you have been chosen for the job, celebrate!

How to deliver effective interview presentations: students' perspectives

We carried out some research with our part-time postgraduate students who had been asked to deliver presentations as part of several job interviews. We asked them to give feedback under two broad areas of:

1   Preparing for the presentation.
2   Delivering the presentation.

We summarize their thoughts and experiences in italics below within the questions we used in this research.

1   Preparing for the presentation

Did preparing for the presentation seem to get in the way of preparing for the interview?

- *Yes, all students thought they had spent more time thinking and worrying about the presentation than for the interview. They thought that they had to be careful not to concentrate too much on the presentation instead of the interview.*

Suggestions:

- Prepare for the interview by researching and learning about the job, the organization and the wider sector in which it operates. Think about possible questions and prepare some suitable answers.
- Now prepare and rehearse the presentation.
- Think about the links between what you have prepared for your presentation and the job for which you are being interviewed. These links could generate questions from the audience so prepare some possible answers with examples.

Which seemed to take the most effort and why?

- *The preparation for the presentations seemed to take much more time than preparing for the interviews. Even for short presentations of five minutes, the presentation still seemed to take quite a long time to prepare.*
- *Students thought they had more control over the presentation whereas they did not think they would have any influence over what questions would be asked in the interviews.*
- *They believed that even though they could think about the possible interview questions and prepare some answers it would be expected that they would need to 'think on their feet' and they also thought the interview panel would accept that too.*
- *They also thought the interview panel would have higher expectations of the presentation than for the interviews. Candidates had been given time to prepare a good presentation so they would need to be well prepared and competent in how they gave their presentation.*

Suggestions:

- Make sure that your presentation is well prepared and rehearsed but do not expect to be word perfect. This will probably create a stilted presentation because you will be concentrating on recalling every word. One student said that in the early stages of her preparation, she had tried to memorize all of the presentation. However, because this took so much of her time, she realized that it was better to rehearse and understand the general content of the presentation and create cards that she could use as prompts.

- Understand and rehearse your content. Create and use clear prompts. This will give a better impression and performance in most interview situations. It will also give you some freedom to 'think on your feet' and adapt something if you need to at the last minute.
- The audience expectations will be high but try to meet these expectations by delivering an excellent presentation.

How did you decide what content to include?

- *Guidelines had been given to most of the students, such as a theme or task on which they were asked to present. They were told how long the presentations should last and whether or not they could use any technology.*
- *Students approached the presentation tasks in the same way that they prepared for an assignment. They did some research and read around the topic. They then listed the key themes of importance and chose which to concentrate on in the time available.*
- *Several students looked for relevant quotations that would enrich the content. All these students tried to set a short presentation within a wider context. They thought this helped to show they understood the topic in relation to this context rather than in isolation.*
- *While preparing their presentation, some students talked about it with colleagues at work, tutors or anyone with useful knowledge and experience. Even though they did not use all of the suggestions given, these discussions helped to make their final decisions about the content and style of the presentation. Discussing the topic with others increased their confidence to present on it.*

Suggestions:

- Read the briefing details very carefully and follow the guidelines given.
- During your presentation you will need to demonstrate your knowledge and understanding of the topic area. When you are given the freedom to choose the topic, select some issues and examples that are current in your professional sectors.
- If you have been given the topic for the presentation, try to make links to current issues. This approach can generate further questions from the interview panel. This will help you to feel more confident when answering these questions.

Did you use any specific skills and methods to create the presentation?

- *All students had delivered several presentations during their academic courses and even when they did not enjoy doing them, they had learned something and used this experience for their interview presentations.*
- *As mentioned above, they approached the task in the same way that they approached assignments: preliminary research; reading into the topic; selecting content and editing this content to fit the time available.*
- *Some students had previously attended public speaking courses so used the skills and knowledge gained from these. Examples included:*

- having a beginning, middle and end to the presentation
- using a prompt sheet of main points
- accepting that in a short presentation you can only make a few points so do not overload it
- make sure you can deliver it in the time available

When PowerPoint was expected, students had rehearsed it, but they also made sure they remembered the content and had paper versions, just in case the technology failed on the day.

Suggestions:

- Use your existing skills and draw on your own experience. The interview and presentation are an opportunity to demonstrate your skills as well as your knowledge.
- Think about some examples of how your academic course has helped to prepare you for employment. Reflect back to your experience when you started the course and what you have learned since.
- If possible, discuss the presentation and interview with a tutor. Suggestions and advice might be useful for looking at a topic from different perspectives.

What advice would you pass on for developing content for this type of presentation?

- *Do not try to fit everything into a short presentation. Try not to think that you need to say everything about the topic in the time available. Stick to a few important points that can be covered briefly or discussed in more detail if there is more time given after the presentation is over or during the interview.*
- *Discuss what you have been asked to do with colleagues. It will be useful to hear about different approaches, even if you do not choose to do them.*
- *Look at any presentations that you or colleagues have done previously, to see if anything can be re-worked to fit the purpose. This saves 're-inventing the wheel'.*
- *Rehearsal is very important. It helps to run through the presentation with someone timing you. Use any feedback they give.*

Suggestions:

- Read the relevant chapters of this book.
- Allow plenty of time to prepare and rehearse your presentation.

2   Delivering the presentation

Were you in a different state of mind during the presentation than for the interview?

- *All the students reported that before the interview date, they felt much more nervous about the presentation than for the interview. However, on the day, they described being more nervous during the interview than for the presentation. Once their presentations had started, they began to relax. They felt much more in control because they had rehearsed and practised as well as they could have during the time available. In the interview they all felt more uncertain and nervous because they did not know what they would be asked or what to expect.*

Suggestions:

- Try to avoid anxiety about the presentation distracting you from preparing for the interview.
- We believe the calmer feelings during the presentation were due to very good preparation so do prepare yourself for the interview stage of the event as well as for the presentation.
- Be totally familiar with the details of your CV, the reasons given for your application and how you see yourself contributing to the job and organization. There will almost certainly be questions about these.
- Prepare several possible questions they will ask you during the interview and rehearse the answers that you will give.
- Prepare a few questions to ask the panel towards the end of the interview. Write them down and ask if you can check them, as you think one or two have been answered already during the event. This will help you to keep some control over the interview.

Tips for successful interview presentations

Finally, after several years experience of assessing presentations and coaching students for their interview presentations, we can pass on a few tips to help you:

Travel light

Don't be a bag lady or man! Think about the impression you give when you enter the room. If you have bags, coats, notes, handouts, it will look like clutter. Try to leave coats and any large bags outside the presentation room. Confine all the papers that you need in one file. Store them in the order that you will use them or at least be familiar with how you have stored them in this file so that you can find each item quickly.

Do not 'hide' behind the technology

You can be trained to use technology. The presentation gives the opportunity for the interview audience to look at you the person, not you the technical operator! This is an opportunity to convince the audience that you are a strong candidate for the job.

Content and structure

If you have been given a free choice of topic, at the start of the presentation explain what you have chosen to cover and briefly give your reasons for this choice in a confident rather than apologetic tone. Give a brief outline of the topic and then show how the presentation is structured.

The beginning: The introduction
The middle: The key points or issues you think are important with examples
The end: The conclusions and any reflections or possible future issues

Close the presentation by thanking the audience for their time, then stand still and remain where you are.

After the presentation

The format of the next stage will vary depending on how many candidates are being interviewed on the same day or on whether the presentation precedes or follows the interview. You could be asked to leave the room so that the next candidate can enter and deliver their presentation. Alternatively, if the interview follows the presentation, the person leading the interview will probably ask you to come and sit down at a table, perhaps facing the panel so that you can answer some questions. Try to take a few deep breaths and move into 'interview' mode. Try not to be too anxious about whichever approach is taken, just accept it.

Conclusions

All these students got the jobs they wanted. Their experience is useful so use what you can from their suggestions. We know that it sounds simple but just try to do your best.

Whatever the outcome of your interview presentation, reflect on this event, think about what you have learned and what can be improved in the future. Nothing is wasted, work for one presentation can bring benefit to another and the experience that you get from doing these will help to increase your confidence over time. We hope that you have found this book helpful. Good luck with your presentations!

Appendix 1   Presenting Numbers Effectively

This appendix focuses on ways of presenting numbers with maximum impact. These guidelines apply to most subjects. However, there may be some specific guidelines available in your own subject area, particularly if it is a quantitative one.

Large images or not?

Are you going to project your numbers as a large image or supply them as support materials, for instance in a handout?

Large images can be used, for instance, using an overhead projector, PowerPoint, flipchart or electronic whiteboard. Graphic presentations like these work best when you want to provide overall summary data, and make an impact. Use a large image when you want to provide an immediate and strong overview. If you do this, you will have to cut some of the detail.

Use standard size images in a handout when you want to refer your audience to more detailed numbers, either within the session or to take away and think about afterwards. Always think in advance about whether or not you are going to use colour. Colour can make your presentation more memorable but too many colours can make it unreadable.

Tables

Use tables for precise values or local comparisons. A well-constructed table is sometimes much easier to understand than a complicated graphic. However, if you are projecting a table, make sure that all the columns and the table itself are labelled and ensure that you show the total number. If your chart shows a percentage, make it clear what the percentage refers to.

Visuals – graphs and charts

Graphs and charts can provide considerable impact and allow you to make very direct comparisons. Always ensure that that each one is properly labelled. You can call your graphics either 'figures' or 'charts' – the terms are used interchangeably. Just be consistent. Label both axes and again, ensure that the total number is shown.

Type A. Bar charts   Bar charts are used to summarize data, and the statistical values are represented by bars. Ensure that any codes are explained. Label both axes and again, ensure that the total number is shown.

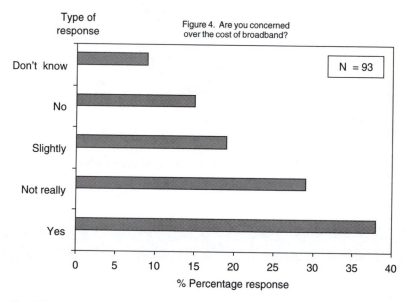

Appendix 1 Figure 1.1   A simple bar chart

Type B. Line graphs   Line graphs are a familiar way of presenting data. They plot data over a period of time, and are therefore useful for showing trends. However, avoid showing too many trends simultaneously.

Type C. Pie charts   Pie charts are often used by students, but they are difficult to use effectively. Pie charts are best avoided unless only a few items are being measured. If used, always keep the slices of pie to a minimum. (See Appendix 1, Figure 1.2, page 156.)

Rounding up and down

When presenting numbers in a graph or a chart, it may be permissible to round numbers up or down to the nearest whole number. Most audiences will prefer you to say 80 per cent rather than 79.81 per cent, unless the difference is critical. You can leave the detailed tables for an appendix in your assignment.

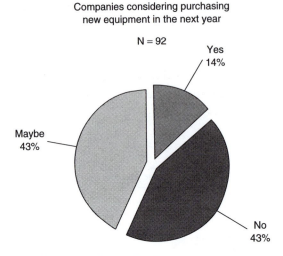

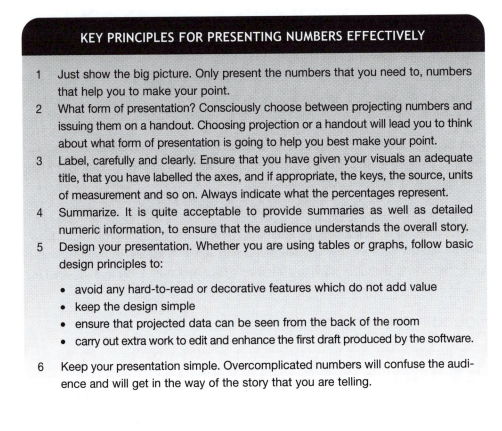

Appendix 1 Figure 1.2 A simple pie chart

Make sure that when all the numbers you are using in your tables have been rounded up or down, they do add up to 100.

KEY PRINCIPLES FOR PRESENTING NUMBERS EFFECTIVELY

1   Just show the big picture. Only present the numbers that you need to, numbers that help you to make your point.
2   What form of presentation? Consciously choose between projecting numbers and issuing them on a handout. Choosing projection or a handout will lead you to think about what form of presentation is going to help you best make your point.
3   Label, carefully and clearly. Ensure that you have given your visuals an adequate title, that you have labelled the axes, and if appropriate, the keys, the source, units of measurement and so on. Always indicate what the percentages represent.
4   Summarize. It is quite acceptable to provide summaries as well as detailed numeric information, to ensure that the audience understands the overall story.
5   Design your presentation. Whether you are using tables or graphs, follow basic design principles to:

   • avoid any hard-to-read or decorative features which do not add value
   • keep the design simple
   • ensure that projected data can be seen from the back of the room
   • carry out extra work to edit and enhance the first draft produced by the software.

6   Keep your presentation simple. Overcomplicated numbers will confuse the audience and will get in the way of the story that you are telling.

Finding out more about presenting numbers

There are many books which detail 'how to' techniques for producing specific kinds of graphs or charts using Excel or similar spreadsheet software. In addition, your institution may well have a specialist learner support section that can help you. Failing that, there are many sources of useful information on the web. For instance, the BBC education website has some helpful guidance, so has the BBC bitesize site (BBC, 2007). The Microsoft on-line support website is very helpful on Excel graphs and charts (Microsoft, 2007).

Bized (2007) Charts: www.bized.ac.uk

BBC (2007) BBC Bitesize: http://www.bbc.co.uk/schools/gcsebitesize/maths/datahandlingih/piechartsirev1.shtml

BBC (2007) BBC Skillswise: http://www.bbc.co.uk/skillswise/numbers/handlingdata/graphs_and_charts/factsheet.shtml

Microsoft (2007) Microsoft Office on-line. Excel: http://office.microsoft.com/en-gb/FX010858001033.aspx

Appendix 2   Copyright and Plagiarism

Copyright

Copyright is a complicated area. In essence, governments often have laws which regulate the way a particular idea or concept is expressed. For instance, you are not allowed to copy the design of a cartoon character such as Bart Simpson nor the logo of a well-known chain such as Nike™ nor a photograph by famous photographer Man Ray, because they are all copyrighted, i.e. protected from exploitation.

Put simply, you are not allowed to reproduce all kinds of materials without permission; this includes music, literary works such as books, magazines, paintings, drawings, videos, downloads from the web, or many designs. The law varies from country to country. For instance, in the United Kingdom and the United States, you are allowed to copy portions of journal articles and books when they are being used for educational purposes. In the UK this is described as being for 'research or private study'. You may be able to copy material for examinations, and possibly for final assessments, but it will depend very much on the law, and on local practice in your institution. Whatever the practice, you must be aware of copyright.

You may have some discretion in certain areas because of the so-called 'Fair Dealing' clauses in copyright law. You are not allowed to copy the whole publication. However you may be able to copy part of it if you are researching for educational purposes, and not for commercial purposes. This permission is for private study only. In normal circumstances, you cannot produce multiple copies of copyright materials for your audience in a presentation.

In the UK, the Copyright Licensing Agency allows additional copying in institutions which have paid for an appropriate licence. Your university or college will have guidelines. Consequently, this Appendix is just a reminder that:

1 You cannot download and reproduce anything you see on the web or photocopy or reproduce anything that you find in a book or magazine.
2 Copyright law is complicated.
3 When in doubt, ask your tutor or a librarian for help on what you can and cannot reproduce.

We have an additional section on copyright images in Chapter 9.

Plagiarism

Plagiarism is different; it is not just illegal, it is cheating. You MUST NOT plagiarize other people's material. Plagiarism means pretending that material you have written is original when actually you have copied it from elsewhere. Most institutions have very clear rules about plagiarism and often take firm action against students who plagiarize. If you copy directly from other sources and you do not put quotation marks round the quotation and provide your source, that is plagiarism and it can get you into a lot of trouble. Similarly, if you 'borrow' other people's ideas using the same language and do not make the original source clear, you could be in trouble.

Your lecturers will encourage you to read a variety of sources and learn from other people's ideas, but not to quote word for word without acknowledging the quotation. Every time that you cut and paste text, you must acknowledge it with a citation.

Lecturers are very good at spotting similar or identical material. An increasing number of universities and colleges are using anti-plagiarism detection software for coursework. So to summarize, please do not plagiarize; it is not worth it and it does not help you to learn effectively. You must make your sources clear, both verbally in your presentation and in any visuals or handouts.

KEY PRINCIPLES ON COPYRIGHT AND PLAGIARISM

1   You must not break copyright law.
2   You must not plagiarize.
3   You must protect yourself against plagiarism and copyright problems.

Appendix 3   Presentation Skills Guidelines

Here are some brief guidelines to help you prepare:

Purpose of the presentation
Understand the assignment and briefing details.
Be completely clear about the purpose of the presentation.
Establish if the presentation will be assessed, how it will be assessed and by whom.
If assessment criteria are available, make sure you understand those too.

Planning
Calculate the amount of time you need to spend on preparation.
Make a plan to research the content.
If working in a group, set up clear communication channels and allocate roles.
Make sure you review your progress; develop a technique for a mid-stage progress review.

The audience
Keep your audience in mind; think about what they will already know about your topic.
Be clear about what they will want from the presentation.
Work out how much audience participation is desirable.

Creating content
Find and select relevant examples to use.
Shape the content into a logical structure that the audience will understand.
Prepare appropriate audiovisual aids.
Edit all your materials to remove errors and make them readable.

Rehearsal
Allow sufficient time to rehearse.
If you are working in a group, practise your individual contributions.
If you are going to use technology on the day, make sure that you have a plan in case it doesn't work.

Learn suitable techniques to reduce tension and feel positive.

If possible, practise with the equipment in advance, in the presentation venue.

Ensure that you can deliver the presentation within the time allowed.

Anticipate and practise possible questions and plausible answers.

Delivery

Make the structure clear to the audience.

Ensure that your breathing is under control.

Remember to maintain eye contact with the audience.

Use PowerPoint or other visual aids to support your talk, but not to dominate it.

Find ways to involve the audience and engage them.

Ensure that you do not overrun your time slot.

When it's all over

Reflect on the event and on your own performance.

Work out what you can learn from the presentation, so that you can improve next time.

Bibliography

Adair, J. (1986) *Effective Team Building*. Aldershot: Gower.

Atkinson, C. (2005) *Beyond Bullet Points*. Washington, USA: Microsoft Press.

Belbin, M. (1981) *Management Teams*. Oxford: Butterworth.

Bell, J. (2005) *Doing Your Research Project: a Guide for First-time Researchers in Education, Health and Social Science.* 4th edn. Maidenhead: Open University Press.

Buzan, T. (2003) *The Mind Map Book – Radiant Thinking*. London: BBC Active.

Cottrell, S. (2003) *Study Skills Handbook*. 2nd edn. Basingstoke: Palgrave Macmillan.

Cyert, R. M. and March, J. E. (1963) *A Behavioural Theory of The Firm*. Englewood Cliffs, NJ: Prentice Hall.

Denscombe, M. (2003) *The Good Research Guide*. 2nd edn. Milton Keynes: Open University.

Diehl, M. and Stroebe, W. (1987) 'Productivity loss in brainstorming groups: toward the solution of a riddle', *Journal of Personality and Social Psychology,* 53: 497–509.

Janis, I. L. (1982) *Groupthink: A Study of Foreign Policy Decisions and Fiascos*. 2nd edn. Boston, MA: Houghton Mifflin.

Janis, I. L. (1989) *Crucial Decisions*. New York: Free Press.

Lowe, D. (2003) *PowerPoint for Dummies*. New York: J. Wiley/Dummies Books.

McCarthy, P. and Hatcher, C. (2002) *Presentation Skills: the Essential Guide for Students*. London: Sage.

Myers, D. G. and Lamm, H. (1976) 'The group polarization phenomenon', *Psychological Bulletin,* 83: 602–27.

Rogelberg, S. G., Barnes-Farrell, J. L. and Lowe, C. A. (1992) 'The stepladder technique: an alternative group structure facilitating effective group decision-making', *Journal of Applied Psychology,* 77: 730–7.

Tuckman, B. and Jensen, M. (1977) 'Stages of small group development', *Groups and Organizational Studies,* 2: 419–27.

Warr, P. (ed.) (1996) *Psychology at Work*. 4th edn. Harmondsworth: Penguin. *(Although there is a later edition of this book, this 4th edition is still useful as different contributors have been used in the later edition.)*

Warr, P. (ed.) (2002) *Psychology at Work*. 5th edn. Harmondsworth: Penguin.

You can find a list of web resources at http://www.sagepub.co.uk/chivers and shoolbred.

Index